Blind Zen

Martial Arts and Zen
for the Blind and Vision Impaired

By Stefan H. Verstappen

Woodbridge Press

Blind Zen,

Martial Arts and Zen

for the Blind and Vision Impaired

Copyright © 2004 by Stefan H. Verstappen

Woodbridge Press

2nd Edition Toronto 2011

Originally published by
Red Mansion Pub
San Francisco 2004

Cover Design: S. Verstappen

All Illustrations by S. Verstappen

ISBN 978-0-9869515-1-0

The author of this book does not dispense medical advice or proscribe the use of any technique as a form of treatment for physical or medical problems without the advice of a physician. The intent of the author is only to offer information of a general nature to help promote a more active and rewarding lifestyle for those with vision impairment. The author does not assume any responsibilities for injures that may occur in pursuing certain exercises. Please consult a physician before engaging in any of the physical exercises.

Blind Zen

Table of Contents

INTRODUCTION   9

WHAT IS ZEN?   13

GROUNDING   19

POSTURE   21
TRAINING EXERCISES FOR POSTURE   26
GENERAL PRINCIPLES OF GOOD POSTURE   26
HOLDING THE JUG   28
HORSE STANCE   29
TAI CHI   32
THE STOP EXERCISE   34

BALANCE   37

HOW WE SENSE BALANCE   39
BALANCE TRAINING   43
THREE POINT BALANCE   44
WALKING THE CURB   45

SENSORY ENHANCEMENT TRAINING   49

PERCEPTION   53
HEARING   55
WHAT THE EARS SENSE   58
TRAINING THE EARS   62
AUDITORY INDEXING   62
AUDIO CALIBRATION   66
EXTENDING HEARING EXERCISE   68
CARE FOR THE EARS   70
OLFACTION   71
HOW THE NOSE SENSES   74
WHAT THE NOSE SENSES   75
TRAINING THE SENSE OF SMELL   76
THE TECHNIQUE OF SNIFFING   79
TRACKING   80

WALKING LESSONS 82

THE SEVENTH SENSE 83

NO MIND 84
THE HIDDEN SENSE 87
TRAINING THE SEVENTH SENSE 89
DETACHMENT 93
QUIET & ISOLATION 96
INNER CALM 98

FEAR 101

THE PHYSIOLOGICAL BASIS OF FEAR 103
TAMING FEAR 108
BREATHING 109
CALMING BREATH 111
ABDOMINAL OR DEEP BREATHING 112
RHYTHMIC BREATHING 113
RELAXATION 116
CONTROLLING TENSION 117
CLASSICAL CONDITIONING 118
RELEASING THE BOWSTRING 120
SYSTEMATIC MUSCLE RELAXATION 121
SYSTEMATIC DE-SENSITIZATION 122
WALKING LESSON 126

SELF-DEFENCE 129

TOUCH SENSITIVITY 130
TOUCH SENSITIVITY EXERCISE 132
ESCAPE FROM STRAIGHT HAND GRAB 137
ESCAPE FROM DOUBLE FRONT HAND GRAB 138
ESCAPE FROM DOUBLE HAND GRAB FROM BEHIND 139
ESCAPE FROM FRONT HAND CHOKE 140
ESCAPE FROM HAND CHOKE FROM BEHIND 141
ESCAPE FROM CHOKE FROM BEHIND [ARM BAR] 142
ESCAPE FROM A HAMMERLOCK 143
ESCAPE FROM BEAR HUG FROM BEHIND [UNDER ARMS] 144
ESCAPE FROM BEAR HUG FROM BEHIND [OVER ARMS] 145

ESCAPE FROM FRONT BEAR HUG [UNDER ARMS]   146
ESCAPE FROM FRONT BEAR HUG [OVER ARMS]   147
ESCAPE FROM HAIR GRAB FROM BEHIND   148
ESCAPE FROM SIDE HEAD LOCK   149

ADVANCED MARTIAL ARTS   151

FORMS/*KATA*   152
SPARRING   159
WEAPONS   166
CONCLUSION   171
AFTERWORD   172
GLOSSARY OF MARTIAL ARTS STYLES   173
BIBLIOGRAPHY   176
INDEX   178
OTHER BOOKS BY STEFAN VERSTAPPEN   181

Introduction

If you gaze at a single leaf on a single tree, you do not see the other leaves. If you face the tree with no intention and do not fix your eyes on a single leaf, then you will see all the many leaves. If your mind is preoccupied with one leaf, you do not see the others, if you do not set your attention on one; you will see hundreds and thousands of leaves.

Yagyu Munenori, *Book on Family Traditions in the Art of War*

The stout bald-headed monk kneeled in the mud gripping his walking stick. He was blind and so tilted his head slightly to better hear his attacker through the sound of pouring rain. His opponent leapt forwards, a gleaming sword raised above his head. The blind monk darted off to the side and stopped. The attacker stopped also, a surprised look on his face, and then fell forward into the mud. A flash of metal reveals a sword blade in the monk's hand. With a flick of his wrist he shook the blood off the blade and slid it back into his walking stick.

This scene was from an old Japanese movie series based on the folktales of Zatoichi - Ichi the blind monk. Ichi carried a sword hidden in his walking stick and roamed feudal Japan righting wrongs and defending the weak from the strong. He was Japan's Zorro but with one major exception, he was blind. This did not seem to hinder his skill with a sword and curiously the Japanese public did not seem to question the character's authenticity. Being a blind man did not detract from what people thought he was capable of. It is true though that Zatoichi was special in another way, he was a martial artist.

I remembered this scene and wondered if it was truly possible for a blind man to learn sword fighting. This was no idle speculation. I had just begun teaching a self-defence course at the local community centre when a woman, Susan, called and asked if I offered private lessons? I replied that I did. Would she have to come to the community centre? - Yes. Then she had a strange request; could I pick her up at her house and drive her to the center? My first thought was that she had an overblown sense of self entitlement, but on a hunch I asked her if she had a disability. There was an awkward silence. I told her not to worry if she was handicapped since anyone can learn martial arts. Then she said, "You probably think this is ridiculous but could I learn self-defence even though I'm blind?" My initial reaction was to say no, but I had just told her that anyone could learn martial arts and I hate making a hypocrite of myself if I can avoid it. In the martial arts, the idea of a blind person learning how to fight is not considered farfetched. Theoretically it was possible, though no one I ever met knew how. So I told her the truth, I didn't know, but if she was willing to try, so was I.

In some martial arts schools, advanced students are taught fighting techniques while blindfolded in order to develop a kind of secondary sensory accuracy. The implication is that when one loses the sense of sight, the other senses will become more enhanced and will compensate for the loss of vision. That is why Zatoichi tilted his head in the rain, to focus on his enemy using his heightened sense of hearing. Japanese folklore tells of how the *Ninja* trained blindfolded until they were able to move about and fight naturally in complete darkness. They were legendary warriors and if Susan was to be successful in learning self-defence she would need to become one.

I arranged to go over to Susan's house for coffee and to assess her situation. I told her I would decide afterwards whether or not I thought I could help. I learned that Susan was thirty-six years old, divorced, and lived alone with her ten year old daughter. She had lost her vision as a complication from childhood diabetes1. Her physical fitness level was poor. Dark haired and about 5' 3" she was approximately forty-five pounds overweight. Her vision was completely absent being unable to distinguish even light from darkness. She had also had a partial liver transplant and as well as several other surgeries. She spent much of her time alone in the house until her daughter returned from school. Susan owned a seeing-eye dog, a friendly golden retriever named Spencer, and with his help she was able to find her way to her neighbour's house,

---

1 Diabetic retinopathy.

but she never ventured further than that. Susan had a collapsible white cane somewhere in the back of the hall closet that she felt uncomfortable with and seldom used.

I questioned her about her other senses, were they more sensitive? Were they able to offset the lack of vision to any degree? Susan thought her hearing to be more acute than when she was sighted, but that she felt there was little advantage to this. No other senses were thought to have become more sensitive or improved. Susan had no training in any practical methods of dealing with her blindness such as instruction on physical fitness, sensory enhancement training, or use of the cane. She was told that classes on how to read Braille were available at the Centre for the Blind but that was a two hour bus ride away and so she declined.

Susan had no previous experience in any athletics and given her handicaps and physical condition I thought it was a hopeless case. I was about to decline to teach her when I asked her the question martial arts instructors always ask new students; why do you want to learn martial arts?

Her answer was a common one - fear. The reason Susan wanted to learn self- defence was because she was afraid, and who could blame her. She lived alone in a rural area with her young daughter, she was a woman, and she was blind. Her fear was not irrational at all, but it was interfering with her enjoyment of life. She dared not go anywhere alone. She had no family and only a couple of friends that would take the time to drive her once a week to the grocery store. The few times she ventured out of the house alone she experienced panic attacks that were accompanied by feelings of vertigo, she described as a spinning sensation as though she were falling.

Okay, I told her we could do something about her fear, after that we will have to see how it goes. What follows is the story of why and how the training methods were developed to teach Susan self-defense, some of the scientific principles I could find that might explain our methodology, and how the reader can use these techniques to train themselves or their blind students. We will also learn a little about Zen along the way.

What is Zen?

"One day in an emotional outburst the master said "How idiotic! Nobody from a hundred years ago is around today. All traces of them have vanished, but forgetting this, we desire trivial things and become planners and schemers. What stupidity."
Suski Shosan, *Warrior of Zen*

Zen Buddhism is a school of philosophy based on the teachings of Siddhartha Gautama who was a prince in what is now India around 500 B.C. One day Siddhartha escaped the luxurious confines of his palace and walked out into the city. There for the first time he witnessed human suffering in all its forms. From that moment on, he renounced his life of privilege and set out to discover the source and cure for suffering. After six years of wandering and ascetic discipline, Siddhartha sat under a *Bo* tree and became enlightened and thereafter was known as the Buddha (meaning roughly "one who is awake") Siddhartha came to three conclusions ; that life is suffering, that suffering is a result of our attachment to illusions, and that to end suffering one must overcome one's illusions. 2

The teachings of the Buddha were passed down from teacher to student. Then, around 475 A.D, a monk named Bodhidharma brought the teachings of the Buddha to China and became the founder of the Ch'an school of Buddhism. The Ch'an school was a blending of Buddhism with the indigenous philosophy known as Taoism. The mythical founder of Taoism was an old librarian named Lao Tzu (circa 5th century B.C.). He is the author of the principle book of Taoism called the *Tao Te Ching*. Taoism taught that a harmony existed between Heaven and Earth and that it could be found by anyone, at any time- all they needed to do was follow the natural flow of nature called the Tao or "The Way." His basic teaching was that the Tao could not be spoken of, for words cannot describe the infinite Universe. Around 1200 A.D. Ch'an Buddhism spread from China to Japan where it is called Zen Buddhism. An often-overlooked point of interest is that Bodhidharma is also the

---

2 This is gross simplification of what is a vast and complex philosophical system, many portions of which are debatable.

founder of China's most famous style of Kung Fu called *Shaolin* (Little Forest) named after the monastery in which he lived and taught. Thus from its very beginning Zen has been closely related with martial arts.3

Principle Practices

The principle exercise in Zen is a form of meditation called *Zazen*. During this meditation one focuses on breathing, relaxation, posture, and awareness techniques similar to those discussed later on in this book. The other principle practice of Zen is just that - practice. A famous Zen master wrote "We don't practice to become a Buddha, when we practice we *are* a Buddha." This is contrary to the more common idea of working towards a goal or reward. In Zen, the work *is* the reward. This is not hard to understand. Much of what we do is equally or more rewarding to us in the doing than in the end result. For most artisans, cooks, artists, engineers, scientists, teachers, parents, there is just as much satisfaction in the application of their skills and talents as there is in admiring the finished products of their handiwork. Because of this focus on 'Putting your all in everything you do', Zen can be applied to any activity and one could just as easily refer to the Zen of Cooking or the Zen of Automotive Mechanics as the Zen of Archery.

---

3 This is the traditional version of history. Some historians suggest that none of the characters, Buddha, Lao Tzu, and Boddidharma, were actual people but rather myths, and that their writings were compilations from many authors over a long stretch of time.

Religion or Philosophy

Zen can be both a religion and a philosophy although neither term would be completely correct. There are numerous inter-school and personal interpretations. Some focus more on religious ceremony, others more on philosophical principles. Therefore, whether Zen is a religion or philosophy depends on whom you ask. Since Zen imposes no religious authority on believers, people of all faiths could learn from it without conflict. For the reader's better understanding, the sense in which the term Zen is used within the following writing is as a philosophical and strategic approach to improving one's quality of life in general, and should not be seen as forwarding any religious agenda.

The Way of the Warrior

Bushido, literally meaning 'The Way of the Warrior', is a code of conduct adopted by Japan's warrior class known as the Samurai that dates back to the 9th century. Bushido is a collection of behavior protocols that emphasize honor, bravery, and ethics similar to the chivalric code of the medieval European knights. Zen heavily influenced Bushido and for most Samurai the two were indistinguishable. The life of a professional soldier in medieval Japan was tough. Zen's teachings of perseverance, self-discipline, and stoicism were well adapted to form the basis of a warrior's creed.

What can these ancient and foreign philosophies offer the handicapped today?

Like the Samurai, the handicapped face hardships and suffering beyond those normally encountered in life. Like the warriors of old, the handicapped may find affinity with a philosophy that provides tools to promote courage, discipline, and perseverance. That the warrior spirit can empower the lives of the handicapped is evidenced in the following quote:

Security is mostly a superstition.
It does not exist in nature nor do children as a whole experience it.
Avoiding danger is no safer in the long run, than outright exposure.
Life is either a daring adventure, or nothing.
To keep our faces toward change and behave like free sprits in the presence of fate is strength undefeatable.
Helen Keller, *Let Us Have Faith*

The Zen masters of old could not have said it better.

Chapter 1

Grounding

Nan-in, a Japanese Zen master during the Meiji era
received a university professor who came to enquire about
Zen. The professor enlightened the monk with his numerous
theories and ideas on philosophy. Finally he asked the
master what he could teach him about Zen. Nan-in
suggested they first have some tea. He poured his visitor's
cup full, and then kept on pouring. The professor watched
the cup overflow until he could no longer restrain himself.
"It is overfull. No more will go in!"
"Like this cup," said Nan-in "you are full of your own
opinions and speculations. How can I show you Zen unless
you first empty your cup?"
Zen Flesh, Zen Bones

The following week I picked Susan up at her house and drove her
to the Community Center for her first lesson. I had booked one of
the small gymnasiums that provided ample open space to move
around without fear of Susan bumping into things. I began our first
lesson with a test known as the Stop Exercise4. In this test students
are asked to simply walk about naturally but when the teacher yells
stop, they are to freeze and maintain the exact position their bodies
were in at the instant they stopped. This exercise helps both teacher

---

4 This rare exercise is described in Ouspensky, P. D., *The Psychology of Man's*
Possible Evolution, Vintage Books, New York 1974

and student to observe the student's habits of movement and identify such factors as balance, tension, and posture.

I explained the exercise to Susan and requested she not use her walking cane. Susan walked around just like most sighted people would if the lights suddenly went out and they were in pitch blackness. Her arms floated upwards and to the sides even though I assured her there was nothing to bump into. Her feet moved forwards along two parallel lines just like those toy robots that walk by shuffling their feet and throwing their weight from one side to the other. While Susan's method of walking was bad, her standing was worse. When she stood still, Susan would lean forwards, hunch her shoulders and drop her head down. It is the posture someone assumes when they know they are about to have a bucket of cold water poured over them. Another curious observation was that the longer she stood still, the more she would start to wobble until she could not maintain her balance anymore and I had to rush to her side to prevent her falling. In daily life when Susan stood still she would need to lean against a wall or hold onto the shoulder of another person to prevent herself from feeling dizzy. The obvious solution, from a martial arts perspective, to Susan's problems with standing, walking, and posture was to teacher her Grounding.

In the martial arts, grounding is a concept that means to become rooted into the earth. This means rooted both physically through posture, stance training, and movement, but also grounded in the psychological sense of being "down to earth" or practical. There is some scientific evidence to support the connection between the physical nature of being grounded with its psychological version. In the 1950's, famed psychotherapist Alexander Lowen[5] was working with clinical neurotics when he noticed that they often had weak and underdeveloped leg muscles. On a hunch, he put these patients on a training regime to improve leg strength. The results showed a dramatic reduction of their neurosis. To isolate the principle involved even further, he put some patients on a physical training program with no additional therapy and they still showed a marked improvement in their condition. Grounding is learned by practicing several exercises aimed at improving one's sense of 'being in this world' as opposed to the feeling of merely observing the world from a distance. For Susan to learn grounding she would need to go back and relearn what she learned thirty-four years ago, how to stand and how to walk. We began with overall posture.

Posture

You will discover how important it is to keep the right posture. This is the True Teaching.
Shunryu Suzuki, *Zen Mind, Beginner's Mind*

When mastering complex skills such as Kung Fu, dance, meditation, and yoga much emphasis is placed on correct posture.

---

5 *Language of the Body*, by Alexander Lowen, Hungry Minds, Inc; (July 1977)

Teachers of these arts spend most of their time correcting student's postures. The instructions for each action are meticulous; the head must be held thus, the hands and fingers in this position, the weight balanced on this point, and so on. Beginners are usually overwhelmed by the complexity and detail involved in correctly assuming these postures and some might legitimately question their purpose. Apart from being more aesthetically pleasing to the eye, why is there such an emphasis put on posture? The answer is that bad posture is the cause of dozens of ailments, and good posture the cure for those and many more.

Improved Health

Man's upright posture is a relatively recent evolutionary development, and there are still a few kinks to be worked out. One such kink is the fragile nature of the spinal column, which has to support the weight of the upper body and the large mass of the head poised precariously at the top of the spine. This structure is vulnerable to many types of injuries and, through improper usage, can be worn down. For example, if you take a handful of coins and stack them evenly one on top of the other they will be able to support a tremendous weight. However, if even one coin is not in alignment, then the stack will collapse under even a slight pressure. This is what occurs with the vertebrae of the spine. Incorrect posture will force the vertebrae out of alignment. Instead of collapsing, the spine compensates by absorbing the pressure into the muscles surrounding the spine and the disks between the vertebrae. Over time this constant pressure from habitually bad posture will cause the deterioration of the disks and eventually the vertebrae itself. By this time the person will usually have become debilitated by severe and chronic pain. Learning correct posture can prevent unnecessary pain and suffering due to chronic back problems.

Improved Balance and Coordination

Posture also affects the way a person moves. Correct posture is aimed at maintaining an internal equilibrium that translates into smooth and relaxed movement. If you are unbalanced, hunched forwards, arched backwards, or leaning to either side, the muscles in the spine, hips, and legs must compensate for this imbalance. Depending on the posture, one set of muscles must contract while an opposing set must loosen. The muscles that have to contract will become exhausted more quickly and are more prone to chronic inflammation and pain. The opposing muscles atrophy and lose their ability to correct the postural tension needed to maintain proper posture. Walking and moving this way will cause pain and exhaustion even after a short while. Correct posture insures that your method of locomotion is the most efficient, reducing unnecessary stress and loss of energy.

Greater Presence

Posture is part of one's body language. Good posture and a solid, fluid method of movement, communicate to the people around you a sense of confidence and strength. This has numerous benefits. In social interactions this will encourage others to have confidence in you, and a willingness to accept your authority. A 'military' posture communicates that you are a presence in this world whose actions have important consequences. In the martial arts, good posture has the effect of dissuading potential attacks. Most criminals look for victims that appear weak and easy to intimidate. Consciously or instinctively they tend to choose victims whose body language communicates a weak and frightened disposition. Good posture sends out signals that indicate strength, confidence, and awareness, thereby helping to prevent an attack. Most criminals seeing someone with such a confident posture would simply wait for a more suitable victim to come by. In this manner posture is a strategy - by preventing confrontation without resorting to violence, by winning the battle without drawing the sword.[6]

Improved Mental Health

Among Yogis and Taoists it was realized that posture and emotion are connected and that each can affect the other. Recently modern

---

6. The importance of posture in self-defense is illustrated in a study done in the United States on the effectiveness of self-defense training for women. Although women who trained in a martial art had only a slightly better chance of escaping a violent situation, it showed that these women had far less chance of being attacked. The study indicated that while women have a 25% chance of becoming a victim of violence, women who studied a martial art showed a less then 3% chance. The explanation for this disparity is thought to be attributed to body language. Interviews conducted with convicted rapists, muggers, and purse-snatchers, showed that criminals usually choose easy targets, people who, through their body language, show themselves to be vulnerable. It is suggested that women who studied self-defense projected a more confident posture and corresponding body language that discouraged potential attackers.

medicine is discovering the same principles and there are several therapies that treat chronic conditions such as depression, pain, fatigue, and a host of other ailments by approaching the problem from a postural perspective first.

The basic premise is that every emotional state elicits a corresponding posture, and vice versa. Early in our development it is the nervous system's state of arousal that triggers the associate posture. Over time, each emotional state and its corresponding posture become linked together so that one can trigger the other through the mechanism of Classical Conditioning.[7] (See chapter 5 Fear) Posture can also be consciously manipulated to trigger a corresponding response in the nervous system. For example, when you are feeling tired and bored you will find your spine begin to sag forward and the head tilt downwards, while breathing becomes shallow and vision narrows. Over years the body memory of this posture becomes linked with the emotional state that elicits this posture. Anytime you start to feel tired, your body will assume more of this posture. However, if you consciously force yourself to improve your posture you will trigger a more energetic emotional state. Initially the body will offer resistance when you try to assume proper posture, but through repeated effort the emotional state will be triggered and then conscious attention to posture can be freed to

---

7. Classical conditioning formulated by Pavlov. In experiments on dogs, Pavlov could cause them to salivate by ringing a bell. He accomplished this by ringing a bell (Conditioned Stimulus) every time the dogs were fed. Food would trigger the dogs salivation which became linked to the stimulus of a bell ringing,

concentrate on other tasks. By teaching proper posture and movement, many people will begin to feel rejuvenated, both physically and emotionally. Correct posture is thus an essential tool to maintain a mental and physical equilibrium, both in training, and in daily life.

Training Exercises for Posture

When posture is perfect,
the movement that follows is perfect as well.
Taisen Deshimaru, *The Zen Way to the Martial Arts.*

General Principles of Good Posture

The basic mechanics of good posture are as follows.

1. Head should be held straight and balanced. Imagine the head being pulled upwards as though a string was attached to the crown of your head.
2. Keep the shoulders down, rounded, and relaxed.
3. The chest should be flat, neither puffed out nor sunken.
4. Spinal column kept straight.
5. Keep the pelvis tilted slightly forward to avoid arching the back.
6. The knees should be kept slightly bent at all times, never lock any joint in full extension.
7. The feet should distribute the weight onto the ground equally along three points of contact: the heel, ball, and ridge or each foot.

Tips for Trainers

When teaching physical movements, there is by necessity, much physical touching. Teaching for a sighted class requires that students watch how the teacher performs any given action. The blind of course cannot watch you, so instead they have to feel you do it. There are times when they need to put their hands on your hips to feel the way your body moves through a motion. Also when sighted people practice they usually have the benefit of a mirror in which to check their posture and receive 'real time' feedback. You can see yourself doing the movements and make changes as you work through the techniques. With the blind, one needs to provide feedback through both verbal instruction and hands-on corrections. There are times when you will need them to freeze while you adjust their posture, by physically moving the student's body.

Before training begins, explain to your students that there will be body contact, but that if they feel uncomfortable with any of the contact or with an exercise then they can stop at any time.

Describe the posture or position first and then make corrections. It is important for students to try to sense the movement they *think* they are making and then afterwards, have them feel the movement that you want them to make. This helps to improve their sense of proprioception or positioning. For example, I often tell my students to relax their shoulders and they think they have succeeded until I come along and physically push their shoulders down. There can be a big difference in what people think their body is doing and what their body is actually doing. After describing the posture you should then ask the student to hold still while you physically reposition their body. Start with the head and hold one hand across their forehead and with your other hand at the base of the skull and correct the position. Hold the head in the corrected position for a moment and ask the student to feel that position. Then adjust the shoulders, arms and hips each time pausing, giving time for the student to make a mental note of the position. This important feedback will assist in learning each of the physical techniques.

Holding the Jug

It is a common misconception that meditation is always done while seated on the floor with legs crossed and eyes closed. But there is another form of meditation practised by Tai Chi adepts that improves posture and involves standing upright. This exercise is called *Holding the Jug* since you stand and hold out your arms as if holding a large jug.

Directions:

- Stand with your feet slightly more than shoulder-width apart with one foot ahead of the other as if taking a step.

- Keep the shoulders down, rounded, and relaxed. Elbows are kept down and close to the body, with the arms

extended forwards as if holding another person in a hug.
Focus your breathing on your body's center of gravity
located approximately in your lower abdomen.

Begin by shifting your weight from one leg to the other a few times.
When approximately ninety percent of your weight is on one leg,
use the other foot to grind into the ground like crushing out a
cigarette. This directs your attention to the soles of the feet. To
maintain balance when moving, the weight should be distributed
equally on each foot through three points of contact with the
ground: the heel, ball, and ridge. If your center of gravity is too far
forward on the balls of the feet, or too far back on the heels, you
will lose balance and solidity.

After shifting a few times stop, and then breathe deeply and slowly
while remaining still in this position for a few minutes. Practise this
exercise three times a week. Do not let the simplicity of this
exercise lead you to underestimate its benefits. Within a couple of
weeks you will feel more solid and conscious of your body's mass,
and you will be able to stand and walk with less fatigue.

Horse Stance Training
Martial arts are divided into two categories known as the External
and the Internal. The External is that which one can see with the
eye, things such as strength, posture, and speed. The Internal

consists of those things one cannot see such as focus, breathing, and balance.

There is a thing called the "Body of a massive rock." By knowing the doctrine of Heiho, one, in no time at all, becomes like a massive rock. No one will be able to hit you. No attack whatsoever will disturb you. I teach this by word of mouth.
Miyamoto Musashi, *The Book of Five Rings*

In the Internal school, stance training is an important technique said to draw energy from the earth in order to become more solid. A traditional demonstration of a master's stance technique was to call on volunteers to attempt to lift, trip, throw, or otherwise budge the master off his feet. Aikido founder Morihei Ushiba, [8] weighing just over a hundred pounds, often demonstrated his mastery of stance training by remaining immobile despite the efforts of much larger and stronger men attempting to shove him off balance. While initially this exercise looks simple, it is in fact the most difficult to maintain since it is type of stress position. The Horse stance gets its name from the appearance of riding a horse.

---

8 *The Essence of Aikido: Spiritual Teachings of Morihei Ueshiba* by Morihei Ueshiba, John Stevens (Compiler) Kodansha International; April 1999

Directions:

- Spread your feet about one and a half shoulder widths apart and bend your knees so that the thighs are at about a 60 degree angle.
- Press the hands together in front about chest height as if praying.
- Use abdominal breathing to focus your attention onto your center of gravity which is located about two inches below your navel.

Practice standing in a Horse Stance twice a day for about one minute and gradually increasing the duration. Initially you will feel strain, trembling, and burning in the thigh muscles that indicate that those muscles are being worked to exhaustion.

In Kung Fu, this is an important exercise. At advanced levels, lower your stance until the thighs are parallel to the ground. In some schools, teacups are placed on the knees to insure that the student does not attempt to relieve the pressure by rising up. You can do the same by using a broomstick. Bend your knees and lower your stance until you can lay a broomstick across your knees without the stick falling off. Just getting into this position is difficult enough and if you can hold the broomstick for three minutes, you will have developed some solid leg muscles and will notice a feeling of strength in your movements.

Tai Chi Walking

Tai Chi Walking teaches proper posture, moving from the waist and hips, and rolling off the feet rather than landing on them. The Tai Chi walking exercise helps to improve a person's method of walking.

Directions:

1. Begin by standing with your left leg forward.
2. Shift your weight gradually onto your left leg and when all your body weight is transferred onto it, bring your right leg forward until it is besides your left foot with the toes lightly touching the ground. Pause in this position for a moment.
3. Step forward with your right leg but do not put your weight on it right away. First touch your right heel to the ground while maintaining all your weight on your rear leg. You'll notice that you will have to bend your left knee a little so as not to immediately throw your weight onto the lead leg.
4. Slowly shift your weight onto your right leg and as you do so you roll the weight from your heel, along the edge of the foot and onto the ball of the foot until the weight is distributed equally along the heel, edge, and ball of the foot.
5. Repeat the same for stepping with the left leg.

1. Left leg forward, Right hand pushes.

2. Transition, right foot paused beside left foot. Right hand withdraws.

3. Right leg forward. Left hand pushes.

Hand Movements

1. The hands move in coordination with the feet and resemble swimming. As the **left** foot steps forward, the **right** hand extends at shoulder level with the palm facing outwards as though pushing with that hand.

2. The left hand is pulled back to the shoulder with the wrist bent forwards so that the fingers point forwards.

3. As you step forward with the **right** foot, pull the lead hand back to the shoulder, while the rear hand pushes forwards with the palm out.

In Karate, this resembles a Reverse Punch, which means that if the left leg is forward then the right arm strikes out and vice versa.

Tips for Trainers

First, clear an area that you can walk along without bumping into things. Tell the student how many steps they can take before having to turn around and come back. In the beginning, have the student focus only on the walking part. You may have to walk alongside and have the student hold onto your shoulder for balance. Check and correct their posture from time to time. Once the student is comfortable with the walking part, have them go through the routine solo while adding the hand movements.

The Stop Exercise

After a few weeks of training in Grounding and Tai Chi Walking it is a good idea to test your student by occasionally repeating the Stop Exercise. The reason for the stop exercise is to prevent old habits from returning. When practicing the above exercises the student is naturally focused on the principles involved, but when returning to normal life, old habits will often return. This simply indicates that the new training has not yet become second nature.

Directions:

Explain to your student that they are to walk around the room at normal speed and that when you yell "Stop" they are to freeze their position without trying to adjust their balance or posture. Observe the student's position when they have stopped and look for improper balance and tension. If you observe a flaw in the posture such as leaning beyond their centre of gravity or holding the shoulders hunched, rather than immediately pointing out the problem, ask the student to sense their position and tell you if they feel that something is wrong, and if so to correct the problem. In this way students learn to rely on their own internal observation rather than the teacher's external observation. Most times they will sense correctly what is wrong and make the correct adjustments. If there is still something that is off balance or out of alignment, then verbally guide the student to sensing the problem. This is known as the Socratic method of teaching whereby the teacher asks questions and the student must arrive at the answers using their own cognition. For example, if you observe a student is still hunching the shoulders ask him or her questions to guide them to the answer. Do you feel tense? Where do you feel tense? If your shoulders are tense what are they doing? With the clues the student receives from your questions they are able to sense and adjust their position which helps train their sense of proprioception. (See next chapter)

Physical Fitness

Standing and walking are the basic components to Grounding but in addition physical exercise and stretching routines need to be practised to improve overall health and fitness.

I began by treating Susan like any other sighted student figuring that, when there was something she couldn't do, we would deal with it when we came to it. Susan was put through the standard boot camp routine of push-ups, crunches, curls, presses, squats, and jumping jacks. This was then followed by a stretching routine common to martial arts training. To my surprise Susan was able to learn the dozens of exercises without difficulty. Sight, as it turned out, was not needed. In addition to improving her physical condition, this training improved her kinaesthetic awareness, giving her the sense of being *in* her body. This is an important feeling to have for it roots us in the present and makes us more alert and receptive. (See appendix A)

Chapter 2

Balance

One day a young samurai approached a revered teacher of swordsmanship and begged acceptance as a student.

"You must do everything I ask you without question." The teacher warned. The samurai agreed without hesitation.

"Go to the Dojo and walk along the edge of the Tatami by placing one foot in front of the other." said the teacher

Perplexed the samurai did as he was told, but after a week of this practice, he became impatient to pick up a sword. After the tenth day, he could take no more and angrily questioned the teacher when they would begin serious training.

"Very well." said the teacher. "Tonight we will begin serious training." That night under a full moon, the teacher took the Samurai up into the mountains until they came to a deep and narrow gorge. Spanning the gorge was a fallen tree.

"Here we begin training." said the teacher. "Cross over the gorge."

"But the tree is too narrow." said the samurai.

"It is much wider than the edge of a Tatami." replied the teacher.

The Samurai jumped up on the fallen tree but as he stepped forward, the dim light and the sound of rushing water caused him to lose his balance. "I cannot cross." said the Samurai.

"Well then, how can you expect to master the sword when you haven't yet mastered walking?" said the teacher.

The Samurai never questioned the teacher again.

Japanese Folk Tale

Integral to the previous grounding techniques is the sense of balance. However, the complexities involved in this seemingly simple sense require a separate program of training. Susan had a poor sense of balance. During the Stop Exercise it was observed that Susan could not stand unaided for more than a couple of minutes without losing her balance. Standing on one foot, even with the assistance of a cane, was almost impossible. Susan's lack of balance contributed to her anxiety bouts in which she believed that her legs would collapse and that she would faint. It was this fear of weakness and fainting which had discouraged her from being more active. Susan was more likely to experience this fear when she was out in open spaces without a solid vertical surface, such as walls or furniture that she could touch and use as a reference. This is similar to what sighted people feel when standing on the edge of the roof of a tall building, uncertain whether their sense of balance would prevent them from toppling over.

Susan's sense of balance was under-developed because she had lost her sight later in life, after her nervous system had already been programmed to rely on visual information for balance. When Susan lost her vision, a large part of her ability to feel balanced was lost too. Those who are blind from birth learn to balance by utilizing the two other senses used in maintaining balance and so are more stable on their feet. Susan believed that her lack of balance was a consequence of her loss of vision. She was surprised and encouraged to learn that there was no reason she couldn't learn to be steadier on her feet. The knowledge that she *could,* greatly improved her ability to learn the drills.

We began balance training with the three point balance drill (see below) while having Susan support herself against a wall. After a two weeks she used a chair for support, then a cane. After a few weeks she was able to balance without support on one foot for several minutes. By this time Susan's fear of weakness and collapse had all but disappeared and her confidence in her own stability and balance was such that she was no longer afraid to be out in the open. In typical Zen fashion, it was the most basic exercises that brought the most noticeable and immediate benefits.

How We Sense Balance

Balance is controlled by a combination of three senses: the vestibular, vision, and proprioception.9 The basic sense of up and down is provided by the vestibular system located within the

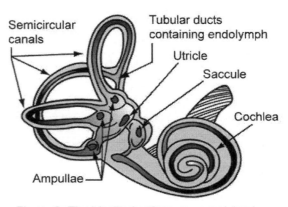

Figure 2: The Vestibular System - semicircular canals and otolith organs

inner ear. It consists of three semicircular hollow tubes that are set

---

9 Sacks declared that the sense of our bodies relies on three things: vision, the vestibular system, and proprioception. *The man who mistook his wife for a hat: And other clinical tales.* Sacks, O. (1986). New York, NY: Summit Books

at angles to each other. These tubes contain liquid that move within the tubes depending on head tilt and movement. Lining the tubes are hair-like nerve endings that, when stimulated by the movement of the fluid, transforms this motion into a neural signal. This provides information on the position of the head, telling the brain when the head is tilted forward, backward, and side to side, similar to a carpenter's level.

While the vestibular system supplies information about head position, it does not communicate the overall position of the body itself. This information comes from two other sources the foremost of which is vision. Vision tends to dominate and override all other senses including our sense of balance. You can test how much vision influences your balance by first standing on one foot with your eyes open, and then with the eyes closed. Most people will begin to lose their balance with their eyes closed. However, vision is not essential to balance and in many cases, its input is detrimental to performing complex movements. For example, gymnasts must learn to suppress visual input during a tumble since its accuracy in determining location of the body in space at any point of a tumble is poor. Instead, the two other senses are refined to produce additional information on speed, trajectory, and distance. Athletes are taught to focus on a spot either on the horizon, or on the ground depending on the technique, and then to *feel* their way through the movement. For example, dancers and figure skaters when performing pirouettes focus their eyes on a point on the horizon. As their body spins, the head and eyes remain focused on that point until the neck will not twist any further, and then the head turns around quickly racing ahead of the body and again focuses on that same spot. If you allowed the head to spin in tandem with the body, the overwhelming visual and vestibular sensations would cause dizziness and disorientation. (Remember when you were a child spinning and falling to the ground and looking up to see the sky whirling around in front of you.) Martial artists use the same principle to execute a spinning kick. The head turns around ahead of the body in order to focus on the target, while the body turns through the movement and executes the spinning kick.

When trainers say you must *feel* your way through the movement, to what "feeling" are they referring. The answer brings us to the third contributor to balance, a vital sense we all possess yet most of us have never heard before – proprioception. One reason proprioception is so little known is that even the scientific community was unaware of this sense until early in the 20th century. 10 This awareness is such a constant touchstone of our experience

---

10 Sherrington (1906) declares that the proprioceptive receptors, the nerves associated with proprioception, are effective at determining changes inside the organism; which is where the term "proprioception" originates. He explains that proprioceptive receptors are used especially in muscles and their accessory organs. Proprioceptive receptors and some receptors in the labyrinth (equilibrium detector located in the inner ear) work together to form our receptive systems. Finally, Sherrington shares that proprioception is responsible for continuous reflexes in skeletal muscles. In other words, proprioceptive receptors are

of being alive that it was simply taken for granted. Proprioception is the information the brain receives from the Golgi tendon organs, which are sensors within the muscles and tendons that measures the amount of tension each particular muscle is exerting. This information enables us to sense physical movement and posture, and tells us how heavy an object is, or how hard to throw a basketball in order to reach the basket. Proprioception is also the sense of being "in" your body. Combined with the tactile sense, proprioception is what tells you that you are part of the world and not an entity living inside your head.

Proprioception was "discovered" when doctors examined patients, who through a rare brain illness, lost their sense of proprioception. Doctors noticed that such patients would lose control of their limbs when they were not observing them. For example, one patient while watching TV was unaware that his arm would of its own volition, float up and over his head. Only when he looked up at his arm could he re-exert control over it and bring it back to rest on the armchair. We all can get dressed, open a bottle of milk, put on our shoes, or execute any one of hundreds of tasks with our eyes closed and it is proprioception that allows us to do this. 11 Thus, it is

responsible for detecting when an area of the body is out of its natural state and prompts the muscles to return the area to a resting state.
Sherrington, C. S. (1961). *The integrative action of the nervous system.* New Haven, CT: Yale University Press.

11 To illustrate the profound effects of proprioceptive loss, Oliver Sacks documented a clinical case of a woman who lost all proprioception. His client lost all proprioception and could not walk without watching her own legs, or talk

important to exercise this sense in training the blind. Proprioception can be improved through both physical activities and exercises, and through the following balance drills. 12

Balance Training

Posture and balance are controlled through the actions of hundreds of small muscles known collectively as stabilizer muscles. These muscles help to direct the movement of the larger muscles and are essential in executing techniques that require refinement and grace. Stabilizer muscles do not develop very much through exercises aimed at isolating and developing the large muscles groups, which is why body builders often appear stiff and wooden. Conversely, figure skaters, dancers, and gymnasts are renowned for their grace and poise attributable to their balance and posture training. Below are a couple of exercises that will improve balance.

---

without listening to her own voice. She could not truly determine if she had a body. The patient could not perform any motor movements most people would deem natural without relying on environmental feedback to achieve the simplest maneuver. Oliver Sacks' clinical story reflects how much the mind depends on proprioception for even the most rudimentary actions not thought consciously considered. *The man who mistook his wife for a hat: And other clinical tales.* Sacks, O. (1986). New York, NY: Summit Books.

12 Rossetti, Desmurget, and Prablanc (1995) conducted research to test if vision or proprioception plays a bigger role in the knowledge of body positions. They concluded that the combination of visual and proprioceptive information assist the subjects in accurately locating the target. Based on their findings, the authors declare that proprioceptive information may weigh more in the localization process than only visual information. Rossetti, Y., Desmurget, M., Prablanc, C. (1995). *Vectorial coding of movement: vision, proprioception, or both?* Journal of Neurophysiology, 74 (1), 457-463.

Three Point Balance

This exercise is similar to those done in ballet, figure skating, and gymnastics. In ballet, this exercise practiced while holding onto a balance rail. A blind student would likewise need to hold onto something solid like a railing or a countertop. As you progress, you can increase the difficulty by switching to a solid wooden cane instead of a railing for balance. Once you feel completely comfortable with this exercise, you can then try to balance using no other support.

Directions:

1. Stand on one leg and raise the other leg up with the knee bent. Hold this position for the count of ten

2. Still keeping your leg up and knee bent, rotate the thigh out 90 degrees to the side of your body, hold for a count of ten.

3. Then lean forward and bring the leg behind you in what ballet would term an *Arabesque*, and hold for a count of ten. Repeat with other leg

Gradually increase the length of time you hold out the leg until you are able to hold each position for one minute. To increase the difficulty level, hold each position with the leg held straight. In addition to improving your balance this exercise also tightens and works muscles in the thighs, hips, and buttocks.

Walking the Curb

This is similar to walking the balance beam in gymnastics, except the beam is a curb. With your training partner find a quiet backstreet or parking lot with a curb and simply practice walking along the curb placing one foot in front of the other. Ensure that the curb section you are walking along is free from obstructions such as poles or hydrants. In the beginning, your training partner should walk along side you so you can hold his or her shoulder for support and balance until you are ready to go it unaided. The technique for placing the feet is similar to the Tai Chi Walking exercise. As you step forward, bend your knees and lower your body to allow the foot that is stepping forward to first brush alongside the edge of the curb. This helps you to feel the layout of the curb. A similar technique is used to walk down stairs. As you step down the stairs, bend your knees and use your lead foot to feel the edge of the step before committing your body weight to the next step.

Another option is to place a ten foot, 2" x 4" beam on the ground and walk across it each day. When you are able to walk across the beam without the least loss of balance, close your eyes and repeat. If you don't have a place for the beam you can always practice walking along curbs if you don't mind the strange looks it attracts.

Tips for Trainers

In working through the above balancing exercises, simply allow the student to hold onto your shoulder for balance. Grabbing or holding a blind person makes them feel uncomfortable and does little to help them balance. Go slowly in the beginning. Allow your student to take as much time as needed while holding onto your shoulder so that they can focus their attention on their muscles and feel their posture and balance. When the student feels confident they can perform the exercise un-aided Stay close by and ready to catch them. It is an important step in moving away from the student since the anxiety of not having you right there to reestablish contact, will sometimes cause students to lose their equilibrium. This seems to depend as much on emotional confidence as it does on the physical act of balancing.

In the previous chapters, we have already begun sensory enhancement training on two vitally important senses, balance and proprioception. These two little known senses are essential to improving the lifestyle and abilities of the blind because they provide a solid foundation and improved confidence in their own body's ability to move and remain solid on their feet. The next chapter will discuss the other two senses traditionally thought to become more acute when a person becomes blind - hearing and smell.

Chapter 3
Sensory Enhancement Training

In feudal Japan, there lived a venerable sword master who decided to test his three highest-ranking students. He brought them one by one to an old temple in the nearby mountains where he told each student the following:

"You have studied with me many years; now let's see if my teaching has been in vain. There within the temple awaits your test. Pass and you will have graduated."

Within the dimly lit temple, the Master had hidden four bandits armed with clubs and instructions to jump anyone who entered the temple. The first student entered the temple and before his eyes could adjust to the light, was surprised and beaten by the Samurai. "I am sorry, you have failed." said the master. The second student entered the temple and sensed the attackers. He was able to deftly evade their attack and defeat them. The student came out of the temple triumphant, but again the master said, "I am sorry, you have failed'. Finally, the third student was brought to the temple and told about the test. The student replied, "But venerable master, protocol dictates that when entering a temple the master must always precede the student, so if you please, I shall follow you in."

To which the master replied, "You rascal, you have learned all I can teach you."

Japanese Folk Tale

The above story, in typical Zen fashion, teaches two subtle points.
First is the effective use of strategy to avoid and evade direct
confrontation. However, there is another point that is often
overlooked; how did the third student know there were four
Samurai waiting in ambush? Was he forewarned by a sixth sense,
or was it one of the common five senses, more finely tuned perhaps?
Did he see subtle traces of their passing? Did he hear their
breathing or the movement of fabric? Did he smell their excitement
and anticipation?

In the Far East, there are numerous tales of legendary warriors who
were able to see the subtle clues that would signal an impending
attack, who could hear the approaching footsteps of attackers in the
dark, or smell the anticipation of those that lay in ambush. These
folktales suggest that true masters were able to sense in unknown
ways things and events inaccessible to the untrained. If it is true,
that they were somehow super-perceptive, then how did they
develop such a talent? Is an acute perception the result of some
sublime spiritual development, or the result of the exercises
involved in these philosophies? Scattered clues in obscure texts
appear to confirm the latter. For example, in the Hindu Yoga
tradition one finds an extended hearing exercise said to be able to
improve hearing. A Buddhist text mentions a candle gazing
exercise said to improve vision, and Japanese Ninja are thought to
have used secret exercises to be able to see in the dark. That martial
artists in the past may have learned to develop their senses further

is a logical assumption. The senses are the windows onto the world. Applied to the art of war, the senses are akin to an early warning system that alerts us to potential dangers. It would make sense that any improvement in this early warning system would enable you to detect a greater number of potential threats, and increase your chances of survival. The question then becomes, can we improve on this sensory system?

We generally presume that what we hear, see, taste and smell is all we are capable of hearing, seeing, tasting, and smelling. However, modern science is rediscovering what past masters had already known, that the senses are capable of sensing much more than we presume. The evidence has always been there. An artist learns to see perspective, contrast, and hue. A musician learns to listen for tone, harmony, and tempo. A masseuse learns to feel for tension, balance, and injury. In every endeavor, one must learn to sense in a new way, to take in more sensum than those that do not follow the same occupation or hobby. So we can all learn to experience more than we experience currently, how can this apply to the blind?

There is a common misperception that those who have lost their sight will find their other senses more acute. This myth was spread partly through movies and television. The Japanese Zatoichi movies, though not well known in the West, did inspire many western films and television shows. These include the blind warrior in the movie "Blind Fury" and blind Master Po from the 70's television series *Kung Fu*, but this is just fiction. Is there any other evidence?

Many traditional cultures attribute super sensory powers to the blind. Throughout East Asia, the blind are thought to be natural psychics, and fortunetellers. They are also renowned for their massage and healing hands. More recently, Helen Keller offers some firsthand accounts of a heightened sense of smell that is remarkable and shows an amazing potential in the humble nose. (See olfaction below). So does all this mean that Susan had heightened senses other than sight? Not at all, actually in Susan's case the reverse was true. Her other senses had experienced a reduction in acuity. So what are we to make of the myth of the blind's super sensory perception?

Part of the answer lies in the late stage in life in which Susan lost her vision. Susan lost her sight gradually beginning in her early 20's until becoming completely blind in her late 30's. Since she was able to see during her formative years, her brain programmed itself to become vision intensive. However, once vision is lost, the brain does not automatically reprogram itself to become auditory or olfactory intensive. In those cases where a child is born blind, the brain programs itself to better process sensory information available from other senses such as hearing and smell. In those circumstances, the other senses will develop to a greater degree than in sighted people.

You can see a similar phenomenon in cases of children born without arms. Many developed dexterity with their feet and legs that could match, and sometimes surpass, what arms and hands could do. However, no one who loses their arms in an accident later in life will ever be able to use their legs to such a degree. Susan having lost her sight later in life likewise will never be able to compensate entirely her loss of sight with her remaining senses. The good news however is that sensory enhancement exercises did improve Susan's perceptions to a remarkable degree giving her greater confidence in all aspects of her life. Let us take a quick look at how the sensory process works and see if there is any scientific foundation for the enhancement exercises of which the ancient's spoke.

Perception: That act or process of the mind which makes known an external object; the faculty by which man holds communication with the external world or takes cognizance of objects outside the mind.
Webster's New World Encyclopedic Dictionary

Perception

There are three processes involved in experiencing the outside world, sensation, perception, and cognition. Sensing is the gathering and conversion into electro-chemical information of external stimuli. Perception is the transference, filtering, and sorting of that information. Cognition is that portion from the wide range of perceptions that is given attention and made aware to our consciousness.

To understand the difference in these processes examine your present condition. You are sitting reading these words while your senses are continuously registering sensum such as, room temperature, background noise, the pressure exerted by gravity on your body, postural information, smells, etc. These various sensum are organized into information that is sent to the brain, but of all these perceptions you are, (or were a moment ago) only paying attention to reading these words (Cognition). At any time however, you can focus your attention on any of the other perceptions coming in such as music or conversation in the background. While reading you where perhaps aware that people were talking, but unaware of the actual content of the conversation, but as soon as you turn your attention to the conversation, understanding takes place. If you turn your attention to your body posture, you may have had a vague perception of discomfort but it is not until you focus your attention to your posture that you are able to identify this discomfort as a result of perhaps holding the neck to one side, or from having your legs crossed for too long. While the senses are continuously providing information, only when you "Notice" these sensations is there cognition. When you focus on a certain set of sensum the brain automatically filters out most of the other sensum, basically turning down the volume of the other senses. Without this automatic filtering process going on deep inside the brain we would be driven to madness by the sensory overload.

So we sense many things but are aware of only some of this information at any given time. Can we become more aware of the other types of information? We can, and we begin with sound.

Hearing

When Siddhartha listened attentively to this river, to this song of a thousand voices; when he did not listen to the sorrow or the laughter, when he did not bind his soul to any one particular voice and absorb it in his Self, but heard them all, the whole, the unity; then the great song of a thousand voices consisted of one word; OM - perfection.
Herman Hesse, *Siddhartha*

In interviewing Susan I learned that her hearing did become more acute since losing her sight but that she felt this provided no real benefits. She heard more sounds but was confused as to both the origin and the location of these sounds. Instead of aiding her awareness of her environment, it actually hindered her awareness with overwhelming noises that often caused feelings of fear.

Strange sounds and noises cause anxiety in all creatures; it is one of our survival instincts. A loud or unusual sound will cause the nervous system to respond with alarm. A sighted person would immediately look in the direction of a strange sound to assess potential danger, but a blind person can only wait for something to happen. Many of us have had a similar experience of anxiety after moving into a new home. Not being used to the different sounds a house makes can keep you up all night wondering if that's the sound of the compressor in the refrigerator, or someone trying to break in the window. There is an exercise for anyone moving into a new house and who might be bothered by strange noises at night, such as single women, that goes as follows.

Before nightfall, turn on all the lights and make a thorough search of the entire home and lock all the doors and windows behind you. This is more for psychological support, making sure that no one could be hiding in the house. Then lie down in bed and listen to all the sounds the house makes. If you hear something you cannot identify, then get up and track down the source of the noise. For example, furnaces often make a knocking sound before turning on. Go and check out the source of the knocking sound, listen to the sound the furnace makes. Do this for every other sound that you cannot identify such as flushing pipes in a neighbour's apartment, the sounds of traffic out on the street, and so on. Once you identify the various sounds in your environment, you are less likely to become alarmed when you hear them late at night.

This method, although developed with sighted persons in mind, provided the clue as to how to train Susan's hearing. Part of Susan's problem was that since her blindness she did notice more sounds, but she was unable to recognize those sounds and had no way of investigating their source. Instead of providing additional information about the world around her, the sounds just made her more confused. The solution is surprisingly simple and very effective. I have coined the term "Audio Indexing" for this exercise and it is described below. This exercise also taught us an interesting principle of all sensory training; that to improve a perception can be as simple as providing clues as to what to look for.

For example, if you play two musical notes a half tone apart such as a C and a C#, they will sound discordant, but they will also create a third vibration known as a pulse tone. Inside the sound you can hear a beat or a pulse. Unless you are a musician or piano tuner, it is unlikely you would have knowledge of this phenomenon and just as likely to never have noticed the third tone. However, once it is explained, it becomes self-evident. I have played music since I was a child but the first time I read of this was when I was an adult. I immediately picked up my guitar and played the two notes and sure enough, there was a pulsating tone. The sound was always there but now I could "hear" it simply because I was made aware of it. Similarly in the following exercises much of the initial improvements are brought about by the mere awareness that we are capable of sensing much more than we originally thought.

In order to be able to judge whether any specific technique can actually improve auditory perception it is helpful to know a little about the mechanics of hearing and understand how the brain processes auditory information.

What the Ears Sense

The ears sense pressure waves that travel through the medium of air or water at frequencies that range between 16 Hz to 20,000 Hz.13 These pressure waves enter the auditory canal and cause a membrane in the ear (eardrum) to vibrate. This vibration is transmitted through a series of tiny bones that amplify the kinetic energy. This energy is transformed into an electro-chemical signal that is transmitted via the auditory nerve to the auditory cortex within the brain where this signal is "heard" as sound.

A curious fact is that the auditory nerves are stimulated by both external vibrations that enter the auditory canal, and internal vibrations transmitted directly through the body. Low frequencies such as bass tones can resonate in the bones of the skull and jaw and vibrate the auditory nerve itself. The skull and jaw act like the

---

13 At around 3,000 to 3,500 Hz, (between F sharp and G in the fourth octave above middle C) the human ear is most sensitive to sound. This is because the auditory canal is about three centimeters in length, which corresponds to the resonance wavelength of sounds in this frequency range. Near this pitch, a standing wave can be formed in the ear canal that requires the least energy for sound to stimulate the ear. This is the frequency of piercing screams and emergency vehicle sirens. (One benefit of this fact is a tactic used in a self-defense situation. A loud piercing yell at this frequency into an attacker's ear can cause extreme pain, disorientation, and even dizziness.)

sounding board of a guitar or violin, and just as the shape of those instruments affect the sound they produce, so our physical structure affects our perception of sound. This is somewhat unusual since no other sense organ can receive direct stimulation of its enervation, its transmission cable. For example, if you could shine a light on your optic nerve you would not see a light.

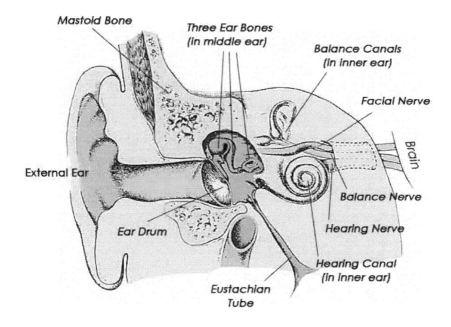

Low frequency sound waves also stimulate the body's nervous system producing an adrenaline/endorphin high. This helps explain why the armies of all cultures have gone into battle beating drums and making loud noises, and why young people like to listen to loud music. The low frequencies act as a stimulant. This may also explain why music and chanting can reduce pain. The auditory signal created by the chanting of a *Mantra* releases endorphins, a morphine-like chemical that inhibits pain, but also literally drowns out pain signals through what is called *cross talk*. All cranial nerves carry a non-steady current, which produces magnetic fields that can both broadcast and receive EM (electromagnetic) waves. Because cranial nerves are densely packed together, when the auditory nerve is stimulated it generates an EM pulse that can be picked up by other cranial nerves through a phenomenon called cross talk. For example, experiments show that even mild and incidental noises cause the pupils to dilate. The auditory nerve can cause a stimulation of the optic nerve. This is why watchmakers, surgeons, and others who perform delicate manual operations are so bothered by uninvited sounds; the sound causes their pupils to change focus thus blurring vision. This is also explains one reason why a warrior yells at the moment of attack, to create an instantaneous and uncontrollable disruption in the opponent's nervous system. This also reminds us that having a quiet place to practice is a good idea since noise is a bigger distraction than you might think. (See next chapter, The Seventh Sense)

In addition, the auditory nerve picks up internal sounds produced by the body's natural processes. These include muscular movement, heartbeat, breathing, blood flow, digestion, and an ambient "static noise" of the nervous system (The hissing sound you can hear when quiet). This allows one to listen in on and monitor certain internal functions like respiration and heartbeat, something again no other sense can do.

A recent discovery offers additional evidence to support the idea of improving hearing. Researchers knew that the sound signal is sent to an area of the brain called the auditory cortex where it is turned into sound. How exactly the process is done is still a mystery but what they have discovered is how sound is sorted. The auditory centres in the cortex have been found to contain a three-dimensional map of the sound space picked up by each ear. What this indicates is that the auditory cortex is highly specialized to accurately detect the direction and position of sounds in the space around us. [14] This specialized ability to pinpoint sound sources would suggest the possibility to fine tune auditory perception more accurately. Whereas the eyes, without moving the head, can detect objects only within a slightly less than 180° field, the ears can detect the positions of sound sources a full 360° acting like radar to accurately pinpoint sources of sound within hearing range. This would be a valuable skill for a martial artist and we devised a simple biofeedback exercise that seemed to work called "Audio Calibration". (See below)

So now we know how hearing works and some of the curious ways in which we hear. The following are the exercises that provided the greatest improvement to Susan's situation.

---

14 Eric Knudsen and Masakazu Konishi (1978) showed that the brain contains a three dimensional grid pattern corresponding to the external auditory fields. From; Smith, Jillyn, *Senses and Sensibilities*, Wiley Science Editions, New York, 1989.

Training the Ears

Learn to be silent. Let your quiet mind listen and absorb.
Pythagoras

Auditory Indexing

The anxiety caused by unusual sounds could best be dealt with using the method similar to the one mentioned previously to alleviate the fears of strange noises when moving into a strange home. The logic is simple; once you know what the strange sound is, it is no longer strange. This was accomplished by having Susan listen to a variety of sounds in and around her home and then have her try to identify what caused them. We would then go together and confirm or correct her answers. Once we had identified the auditory landscape within her home we ventured further going to different places and identifying specific sounds. For example, in walking down the street if I saw a squirrel scurrying in the bushes I would stop and ask Susan to identify the sound. Then I would confirm or correct her answer. While sitting on a park bench I uld have Susan try and identify each of the surrounding sounds, such as children playing, dogs running, a fountain, and so on. In this way Susan quickly became familiar with the sounds within her local environment.

Susan lived on the edge of a small town and she wanted to be able to travel to the local grocery store on her own. The store was only a few blocks from her home but she had been too uncertain of herself to dare the trip on her own. Those of us who have never been without sight can hardly imagine what an enormous task walking a couple of blocks to the store can be. First you have no sense of direction, so which way do you turn first? If we follow the sidewalk how will you know when you come to a break that you are crossing the road or crossing a driveway? How many driveways or roads would you need to cross before arriving at your destination? These are directions no one could possibly provide you unless they went personally with pen and paper and wrote out almost every step you needed to take.

The solution is to take what I called a 'Walking Lesson'. This is simply walking the route to the store while questioning Susan and confirming or correcting their answers. This provided real-time feedback of not only *what* those sounds were, but also *where* those sounds originated. Susan and I walked to the store and as we walked I would identify the different sounds we encountered. After a couple of trips Susan had become familiar with the auditory landscape involved in a trip to the store. The questioning evolved to the point where she could accurately estimate her current position along the route to the grocery store.

For example:

Author: "Which direction is the grocery store? "

Susan: "That direction" (Pointing)

Author: "How do you know?"

Susan: "Because the store is on Main Street and most of the traffic sounds come from that direction."

Author: "How far away are we now?"

Susan: "About two blocks from the store."

Author: "How do you know?"

Susan: "Because we are just passing the gas station and I can hear the sounds of compressed air tools and gas pumps."

This exercised provided two enormous benefits. First, it alleviated many fears by helping Susan to understand the source and nature of hundreds of previously unidentified sounds. She learned what sounds were not threatening such as squirrels, kids playing, and various sorts of machinery, and sounds that might be potentially dangerous, such as the sound of approaching automobiles or footsteps walking too closely behind.

Second, the walking lessons helped create not only a mental picture of Susan's hometown, but also created what could be termed an auditory map. This is an important factor in the Susan's ability to orient herself. Studies show that our ability to navigate our environment is largely dependent on our knowledge and recognition of landmarks. 15 For sighted people the landmarks we use are all visual. We know where we are because we recognize our personal 'landmarks' such as the corner store, the office tower, the city park, the mountain in the distance, the river, lake or

---

15 Gibson, J. J. 1979. *The ecological approach to visual perception*, Boston: Houghton Mifflin.

coastline. Susan had trouble getting around because she had no landmarks by which to navigate. However, through walking lessons we discovered there were audio landmarks that could be almost as reliable as visual landmarks. These included roads and highways, shops and gas stations, schools and industrial buildings, all sources of consistent sounds that are easily recognizable. Others were more subtle such as the sound of the creek running through the center of town and the sound of the breeze through the branches of trees that lined the older streets in town. These auditory landmarks combined with the olfactory landmarks (see next chapter) were able to give Susan a fairly accurate idea of her location anywhere in town.

Tips for Trainers

In true Zen fashion, the teacher during this exercise must also become a student. An important element in this exercise is to ask detailed questions and provide similarly detailed answers. This requires the trainer to also focus on his or her auditory information and to listen and try and identify sounds that most people would overlook. The trainer must become one with the student to hear what the student hears and then to provide visual information becoming the student's eyes. This takes a little extra effort on the trainer's part but you will also be rewarded with enhanced auditory perceptions of your own.

A hypnotised person could hear a constant hissing sound at 230 yards, although non-hypnotized people typically could not detect the sound until they were within 30 yards of the source.

Eugene Marais, *The Soul of the Ape*

Audio Calibration

For this exercise the student stands in the middle of the room and imagines him or herself to be at the centre of a clock face: directly to the front would be Twelve O'clock, directly behind is Six O'clock, ninety degrees to the right is Three O'clock and so on. This is similar to positioning lingo used by fighter pilots except, whereas in the case of aircraft the clock position indicates positioning on a vertical plane (i.e. above or below), the positioning is plotted on a horizontal plane, (i.e. in front and behind).

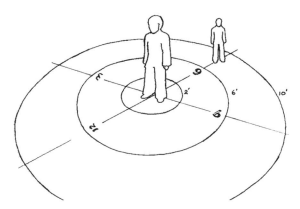

The trainer moves about stopping at random and calling out "Now". The student must then guess the direction and distance or range of the trainer's position. For example, if the trainer is standing directly behind the student the correct answer would be; "Six O'clock/six feet". When a correct answer is given the trainer answers in the affirmative, if incorrect, the trainer would say the correct answer so that the student can associate the correct answer with the immediate auditory experience. When the student is able to guess correctly nine out of ten times, you can move to the next level of difficulty.

This time the trainer moves around the room quietly and the student calls out every ten seconds "Stop". The trainer does not answer. The student must again guess the correct position and the trainer corrects or affirms as above.

Tips for Trainers

Instruct your students to not only listen for sounds that are there but to listen for sounds that are not there. One way to tell when someone is coming into close range is by detecting the muffling of the ambient background noise. As the approaching body absorbs this noise, it casts the auditory equivalent of a shadow. One senses a hole, an absence of sound, coming from the direction of the other person.

Bathe in the centre of sound, as in the continuous sound of
a waterfall. Or, by putting your fingers in ears, hear the
sound of sounds*.*
Soch-anda Tantra, *112 Ways of Consciousness*

Extending Hearing Exercise

This exercise can be practiced in a variety of settings and requires that you only assume a comfortable sitting position. This exercise trains the ability to listen to sounds coming from a specific distance while ignoring all other sounds. This involves the filtering and selection process in the brain and it is quite extraordinary that we have such ability. It is not listening to which sounds are loudest, since distant sounds may be louder than nearby ones and vice versa, but it is listening to specific sounds which originate from a specific distance and direction.

Again imagine being in the centre of a circle but in this case imagine concentric rings emanating outwards at fixed distances. First listen to the all the sounds originating within a three foot radius, mentally ignore other sounds even though they may be louder. It is possible to consciously reduce louder sounds to the background while focusing on the sounds within a particular range. If you are outdoors at this range you typically hear crickets, or mosquitoes, the wind through the grass, a leaf blowing along the ground. Next expand your hearing range to twelve feet and concentrate on the sounds found within this range. These could include the rustle of leafs in the trees, a chipmunk scurrying along a branch, a child on a swing. Be sure to listen to sounds that come from the front and back and from every direction. Identify and briefly focus on each different sound.

Continue to expand the ring in increments of various distances that you can decide on as you go through the exercise. Sometimes you may listen for sounds coming from a certain distance and there are no sounds originating there. That happens quite often and you just continue to move to the next largest circle. Eventually listen to most distant sounds, such as the sound of the surf crashing onto the beach, the sound of running water, a lone train whistle far away, or the distant roar of the city. [16]

In Susan's case after we had created the auditory map through the walking lessons she used the map in her extended hearing exercise. By sitting quietly in her backyard she could extend her hearing outwards from her home, to listen first for the occasional car that drove along her street. Then to the children playing in the schoolyard three blocks away, then on to the gas station she passes on her way to the store, finally listening to the distant sounds of traffic on Main Street several blocks away.

16A similar exercise is described in the book on Indian yoga called Visuddhimagga (The Path to Purification) Buddhagosa, Trans. b. Nyanamoli, Gunasena & Co.

By becoming familiar with the sound of one's environment you are better able to notice changes in the audio landscape. This awareness can be a life saver. For example, could you tell the difference between the sound of a prowler walking around your home, and the rattle of leaves from the wind? Learning the layout of your audio landscape can provide warning signals to potential dangers.

Care for the Ears

As color and beauty are food for the eyes, so music is food for the ears. Researchers have discovered that the right kind of music, played under the right circumstances, can help increase attention span, improve physical coordination, reduce tensions, boost self-esteem, aid learning and memory, and provide physical and emotional relief from disease and injury. This helps explain the universal appeal of music. Classical Chinese and Japanese warriors greatly admired the ability to play a musical instrument. The instrument of choice was the flute, both for its nostalgic and melancholy tones and its lightness and portability. While listening to recorded music is adequate to the task, playing a musical instrument oneself provides additional training in rhythm and harmony, skills useful to martial arts training.

The ears also benefit from rest from noise. The best time to rest the ears is when sleeping. Try to insure that your bedroom is as quiet as possible. You may want to lay down some rugs and hang heavy curtains over the windows to reduce noise. Finding a quiet place of refuge outdoors is also a good way to give the ears a rest. Loud prolonged noise can cause damage to the ears, alter moods, reduce learning abilities, and increase blood pressure. Long-term exposure to loud noises can even lead to deafness.17 The ancient sages knew the importance of living quietly and that silence is golden.

Olfaction

The nose, for example, of which no philosopher has ever spoken with veneration and gratitude - the nose is, albeit provisionally, the most delicate instrument at our disposal: it is an instrument capable of recording the most minimal changes of movement, changes that escape even spectroscopic detection.
Nietzsche, *Twilight of the Idols*

Many types of animals perceive their world largely through their sense of smell, in contrast to humans who perceive largely through sight. We can get an idea of what their world might be like from a few rare cases of humans with unnaturally enhanced olfactory abilities. Usually caused by a brain tumor or other brain dysfunction, people who have hyperosmia, (hyper-smell) describe how detailed and precise the sense of smell can be. They could

---

17.Auditory Fatigue occurs after the ears have been exposed to loud continuous noise. This raises the auditory threshold meaning tones would have to be louder in order for you to hear them. It can take several hours or several days for the threshold to return to normal. Evans 1982. From Sensation and Perception, Margaret W. Matlin.

distinguish friends and acquaintances by smell even before seeing them. Some could smell emotions such as fear, contentment, and happiness. Others could recognize every street, every shop, every building by smell, and find their way around their native towns and cities infallibly by smell alone.18 Other rare cases include people who have developed a natural sensitivity to smell as in the case of Helen Keller. After losing her sight and hearing at the age of nineteen months due to an unknown illness, Keller had only the chemical senses (small and taste) and touch with which to experience the world. She found the sense of smell the most valuable. In her writings, she recounts how she could tell a person's occupation by their smell. She was able to smell what she called "personality" smells that everyone gave off. She noted that interesting and unusual personalities had a more distinct odor, while a lack of odor indicated a less entertaining or lively personality. She enjoyed visiting old country houses where she could smell "layers of odors" left by generations of families that had lived there before. These examples show beyond a doubt that an acute sense of smell could provide a great deal more information about the world than we could have imagined possible. However, the above cases are unique accidents of nature, what can the average nose do?

18."When I went into the clinic, I sniffed like a dog, and in that sniff recognized before seeing them, the twenty patients who where there. Each had their own olfactory physiognomy, a smell face, far more vivid and evocative, more redolent, than any sight face." *The man Who Mistook His Wife For A Hat*, The dog beneath the skin, Oliver Sacks.

Even without hyperosmia, the average person can detect a lot of information by smell. For example, if you visit a friend in the morning, can you tell if he or she is cooking breakfast, and if so what? Bacon and eggs, French toast, coffee? Most people would be able to answer these questions faster by having a quick whiff of the air than by looking around. If you were blindfolded and taken to any number of locations such as, or a downtown city street, hospital, library, or factory, could you not identify the location almost immediately by smell alone?

Studies have shown that men and women alike are able to tell by smell alone whether a male or a female wore a piece of clothing. Special Forces veterans who fought in Vietnam recall that several days before going into the jungle they would have to change their diet since the typical meat rich diet of westerners produced a distinct body odor that gave away their presence to the enemy.

The subtle information received through the olfactory sense may be the source of some previously unexplained sensory phenomena. Dog trainers know that dogs can smell fear and that this smell is why nervous people seem to spook dogs. When people have a gut instinct that something is wrong, could this be because they smell fear? In such instances, we may be processing chemical stimuli in some primitive mammalian portion of the brain not readily accessible by our immediate awareness. Subconsciously we recognize certain odors for what they are, yet this perception does not reach our awareness directly but does so through the subtle medium we can only describe as a hunch or a "gut instinct".19

There is ample evidence that the nose can provide more information about our world than we might imagine. The question was could Susan's olfactory sense be improved and would it help her to better understand what was happening in her environment? To try and answer this question we need to understand the mechanics of smelling.

How the Nose Senses

The sense of smell is anatomically simpler than the other senses. The olfactory receptor cells protrude directly into the environment from the olfactory bulb of the brain. Stimuli in the form of airborne molecules enter the nose and find their way to the olfactory mucosa, which is a sponge-like tissue, covered in mucus that is located behind the nose. Imbedded in the mucosa are nerve receptors that pick up floating molecules and fire a neural signal to the olfactory bulb that acts like the retina of an eye.

The information is then sent to the brain through two different routes. One through the thalamus, where all senses synapse, and the other through the amygdala, hippocampus, and hypothalamus, all

19. An example of odor affecting the body's biorhythms can be found in women living together where is has been shown that smell is the factor behind the phenomena of women's menstrual cycle synchronizing when living together. Martha McClintock (1971) *Sense and Perception*, E. Bruce Goldstein, Wadsworth Publishing, Belmont, Calf. 1989.

structures deep inside the brain which regulate feeding, drinking, and reproductive behavior. Both circuits meet in the orbit frontal cortex, an area in the frontal lobe just above the eyes. Unlike vision and hearing, there is no area of the brain devoted exclusively to processing olfactory sensation. The perception of smell is distributed over the entire brain, an indicator of this sense's ancient origins.

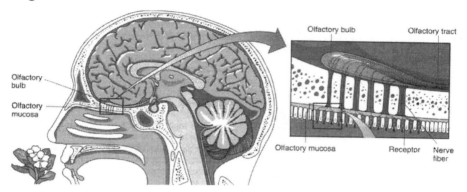

What the Nose Senses

The sense of smell has fewer limitations than the senses of sight and hearing. Vision needs a direct channel of light (vision in darkness is not possible), while hearing can be obscured or baffled, and both are immediate. Smell requires only a molecule to enter the nasal cavity, and these can linger for years making smell less constricted by time. The human sense of smell is so keen that it can detect the odors of substances even when they are diluted to 1 part to 30 billion. The senses of smell and taste are known collectively as the chemical senses since they respond to chemical stimuli suspended in the air and liquids. However, the sense of smell is 10,000 times more sensitive than taste.

The olfactory receptors can discriminate thousands of different airborne chemicals and as many as forty thousand different smells. Organic carbon based substances make up the majority of these smells. (Most inorganic substances we find odorless except fluorine, chlorine, iodine, bromine, and phosphorus). We can also smell ozone (three atoms of oxygen combined) and compounds such as hydrogen sulphide, sulphur dioxide, nitrogen oxide, and ammonia. Most of these odors we find irritating and some even stimulate the trigeminal nerve in the face causing tearing and irritation of the nasal passages. (The reactions caused by pepper spray and mace.)

Training the Sense of Smell

Were all things smoke, the nostrils would recognize them.
Heraclitus [20]

Modern man is seldom cognizant of information derived from smell. One reason may be that cultural sophistication places less importance on olfaction. A keen sense of smell is usually associated with animals and may unconsciously be seen as a

---

20. Quote from: Le Querer, Annick, *Scent, The Mysterious and Essential Powers Of Smell*, Turtle Bay Books, New York, 1992,

primitive sense.21 By ignoring this sense however, we lose an important and possibly lifesaving source of information about our environment. In the animal kingdom, the sense of smell plays a crucial role in survival by providing information on everything from food sources, and predators, to breeding and social interaction. While not as precise as say a dog's nose, the human nose is no less sensitive to smell. Both a dog's and a man's olfactory receptors can be stimulated by a single molecule. (A dog's nose is more receptive to a greater variety of smell perceptions due to there being a greater number of nerve receptors in a dog's olfactory mucosa, 1 billion compared to 10 million for man.)

Under laboratory conditions, using hundreds of bottled scents the human nose can learn to identify up to 5,000 odors. The key is simply learning to `recognize' the smells, to make the connection between olfactory sensation and knowledge of the stimuli's source. The best way to improve olfaction is through experience, observation, and simply becoming more aware of the smell of things.

To improve your sense of smell, simply make it a habit to stop and sniff the air more often and try to make predictions based on what you smell. For example, when coming home, the smell of soap and

---

21.Odor has been often linked with illness and thus forms the motivation behind the western obsession with deodorizers, sanitizer, disinfectants, air fresheners, and perfumes to name a few.

dampness would suggest someone has taken a bath or shower. An unfamiliar smell of aftershave and perfume might indicate that you have guests. When going to the club or gym try to smell who has been training. One person may use too much bleach when washing his uniform and so smells like chlorine. Another eats too much pork and has a sharp salty smell, or eats spicy foods that leave a scent of garlic.

When outdoors use your sense of smell to tell you when the weather will change, such as the smell of moisture before it rains or ozone before a lighting storm. If hiking through the forest try to smell the location of rivers and lakes, roads and highways, and farms and cooking fires. Every city, every type of terrain, and even every season have their own distinctive aroma that you can learn to recognize.

The only known way for improving olfactory sensitivity was simply by increasing one's awareness of it. I suggested a training regime whereby every time Susan, entered a room, or met with people, she would pause and discreetly sniff the air. With trial and error Susan was able to garner additional information about her environment. These included; the ability to detect the sex and approximate age of people from a short distance away, whether a person has been smoking, drinking, working, what they have been eating, and personal hygiene. This was helpful in public situations such as smelling to determine if it was a man or a woman that just got on the elevator, or if the `salesman' at your door smells intoxicated or unwashed. Sighted people can see if a stranger is scruffy, seedy, or intoxicated, but to a blind person he is just another voice, until you sniff them out.

The Technique of Sniffing

Studies show that closing the eyes can improve smell memory.[22] This again shows how much vision overrides other senses and it makes sense that the blind would naturally become more aware of smells. To sniff, begin by closing the mouth and focus your attention on the spot between the eyebrows that corresponds to the location of the olfactory bulb. Relax and take in a couple of short, quick inhalations through the nose and cut off the air intake suddenly without exhaling. This allows the suspended molecules in the air to remain longer near the olfactory mucosa thus increasing the likelihood of penetrating the mucus lining.

Improving the sense of olfaction requires a variety of stimulation. We know this from recorded cases of under-stimulation, such as when constantly exposed to only a single odor, which has been shown to cause degeneration of olfactory acuity. People who work in a chemical rich environment will lose the sensitivity to such odors. Smokers seldom notice their own tobacco smell, fast food employees no longer notice the smell of fried foods and so on. The way to counteract this degeneration is to expose oneself to, and

22. See, Clair Murphy and William Cain, 1986.

consciously sniff, a variety of odors. Have fresh flowers or plants in your environment, smell your food before eating. Smell fruit and vegetables, new clothes, houses and automobiles before choosing which to buy. By becoming more aware of smells and seeking to identify the odors of things will stimulate and improve this curious sense.

Tracking

Probably one of the foremost concerns of living alone and being blind is that of fire. Who has not caught the whiff of smoke and felt the sudden fear that a fire might have started somewhere in the home? To address this fear we invented an exercise called tracking and it is just as it sounds - tracking something down through the sense of smell just like a bloodhound.

Begin this exercise in an enclosed area like a home or gymnasium. Have your student cover their ears or put cotton balls in them to exclude auditory information. We need to isolate the sense of smell exclusively for this exercise and so try to insure that your student does not hear you moving about.

Ask your student to then count to thirty while you go to another spot in the room or another room in the house. There light and extinguished a match. After the count of thirty, the student is to make their way through the house until they find the room or area where the match was lit.

Most people will have little difficulty in finding the correct room. It is important to use a lit match since the smell of smoke is one of the greatest concerns. Once you experience how quickly and accurately you can track down the source of smoke, the more confident you will be in your ability to smell potential fires and to know from which direction the smoke is coming from. With this information, a blind person could better detect and escape from fires.

The next stage in Tracking becomes more difficult. Take a can of air freshener and spray some in the air so that the student can identify the scent. The trainer then sprays some of the air freshener on his or her clothes. The student is again told to cover their ears and count to thirty. The trainer quietly goes to another room in the house or area of the gym. After the count of thirty, the student tries to track down the trainer by following the scent of the air freshener. Again, most students will have little difficulty in tracking down the trainer.

In the final stage, the exercise is the same but this time the trainer does not spray his or herself with the air freshener. The student must track down the teacher by following the teacher's own natural smell. Each of us has a chemical signature made up from various odors we emit. These include the soap you use, the shampoo, underarm deodorant, what type of detergent we use to wash our clothes in, as well as the natural body odors we all give off through our skin and breathing. The student must now identify more subtle odors and be able to track the weaker scent trail left behind by the teacher. With practice, students will develop a high success rate in tracking down the trainer, and other people as well.

Walking Lessons

Just as in the previous chapter on auditory indexing, so the sense of smell can also be used to orient oneself in the environment by providing known 'landmarks' by which to navigate by. In Susan's walk to the store, she would pass some pine trees the neighbors had planted in their front yard. The smell of pine is easily recognizable and was always in the air near that particular house. This becomes an olfactory landmark, a constant source of information about your geographical position. As we came to the street, she would begin to smell the odor of exhaust fumes. Passing the gas station, she could smell gas and oil. All these olfactory sensations helped to confirm the auditory sensations as well and solidify her knowledge of where she was.

Chapter 4
The Seventh Sense

Researchers are detecting another deeper sensory
apparatus; if the conscious mind is somehow impaired, it
seems a secret array of senses in the unconscious may go to
work. Thus blind people may sometimes "see" a flash of
light, brought to them, some scientists believe, along little
used, vestigial pathways in the brain.
The Mystifying Mind, Library of Curious and Unusual Facts

In the Zatoichi movies the blind monk is portrayed as being able to duck and block sword strikes. Chinese sword and swashbuckler stories often include a scene in which the hero is blinded by trickery and yet is able to block and dodge any number of attacks. Even the Star Wars movie shows the hero learning how to block attacks using a sword while blinded by a helmet's face shield. These images portray being blind not as a handicap but almost as bestowing superhuman powers of perception, the ability to read minds and know an opponent's intention before even the opponent knows himself. We have previously learned about the possibilities of how the senses of balance, hearing and smell could be enhanced or improved but could these prove useful in hand to hand combat, or is there another 'Sixth' sense we don't know about? The answer is both yes and no.

Research into parapsychology has yielded little proof of the existence of psychic powers in humans. I believed that it would be almost impossible for a blind person to be able to dodge random sword strikes or block punches. Yet despite the lack of evidence of extra sensory perception, there are times in which something more seems to be going on.

For example; I proposed to Susan that the last five minutes of each lesson we do some sword fighting just for fun to which she happily agreed. I had two soft padded sticks and I gave one to Susan and instructed her on the four blocking techniques to use. Then I told her that I would attack, slowly at first, by swinging strikes to her head in one of four directions. Statistically there would be 25% chance of blocking correctly. Yet she blocked more than half the attacks. What was more remarkable was how often she knew *when* I attacked. I randomized the time interval between swings so that she would not get used to anticipating the attack as following a predictable rhythm. How was Susan able to guess when the strike was coming?

No Mind

In the Zen school of thought, much has been written about a level of consciousness called `No Mind'. It is often described as a state of mind in which the intellectual function of the brain is suspended and the body is run by instinct alone. Among martial artists it is the seasoned fighters that often experience this state. It is one in which you just *know* what your opponent will do next and your timing is almost perfect. From the point of view of novice fighters, a seasoned veteran's ability to anticipate and evade attacks may seem almost supernatural. However, to react without conscious thought, which is too slow for combat anyway, but instinctively, is actually quite a common ability. It just looks more impressive when applied to martial arts than to say, doing the laundry, or driving a car, although in principle there is no difference between the two.

We have to trust in that perfect unadorned perception. The very mind that wants to control things is the mind that's caught up to begin with. When you're caught up, you have fewer possibilities. Your mind can manifest in more ways if you keep it from taking form.

Takuan Soho. Letters to the Swordsman

Let's make an analogy to the game of billiards. If we were to take two people with no previous experience with billiards and train them separately. The first person we train by teaching the mechanical principles of the game such as angular geometry and Newtonian physics, and we provide technical data such as the weight and measurements of the billiard balls, table, and pool cue, etc. But this person is never allowed to actually shoot a ball. With the second person we explain nothing about the technical aspects of billiards, but instead simply allow that person to shoot balls every day. After a few weeks of such training the outcome of a match between the two would not be in doubt. The person who spent time shooting balls would easily beat the person who spent time studying the physics and mechanics of the game. The first person would be restricted to using the intellectual part of his mind. The second person would not be using his intellect at all, he could be said to be using No Mind. 23 Real world experience is superior to intellectual knowledge only. Through experience something is developed that is different from our ordinary intellect. Tapping into this other state of awareness is what Zen practise attempts to do. There is still one more sense that we have not mentioned that may be related to No mind.

Results of tests on memory show that a clandestine mental operative sees and remembers when the conscious mind does not. Called covert awareness it helps out when other senses fail, it also reinforces existing mental functions especially the way humans make decisions known as gut feeling - the hunch.
Stanislav Grov, *The Holotropic Mind*

---

23 "Motor Memory; is the neurological term for behavior that becomes automatic after learning. It is a commonplace observation that any performance, like playing tennis or the piano, even giving a speech, is impeded if you try to think about it. Thinking about what you are doing degrades your ability to do it. Cytowic, Richard E. M.D., *The Man Who Tasted Shapes*, Jeremy P. Thatcher/Putnam Books, New York, 1993,

The Hidden Sense

As we learned from our discussion of how perception works we know that the majority of sensum never makes it past the filtering stages to our consciousness. What becomes of all that information? Well it seems that these 'unconscious' perceptions mingle and merge and create a synthesised sense that is composed of all sense impressions but which seldom makes itself known to our consciousness except in people born with a rare condition known as synesthesia.

The word *synesthesia* means, "Joined sensation" and shares a root with *anesthesia*, meaning "no sensation." It occurs in 1 out of 25,000 individuals and is a condition in which the different senses somehow become jumbled together and trade characteristics. It is *"…the involuntary physical experience of a cross-modal association. That is, the stimulation of one sensory modality reliably causes a perception in one or more different senses."*

For example, persons with this rare capacity seem to hear colors, taste shapes, or experience other equally bizarre sensory perceptions. A *synesthetic* might describe the 'color' of a piece of music, or recognize a smell by its 'texture', or, feeling the material of a sweater detects the "sound" of the fabric as well. These sensations are experienced as being projected outside the individual. In other words, the sense of synesthesia feels just as real as any other sense and not as some hallucination or image inside the mind.

87

When a synesthetic says he or she can *feel* the color red they experience it as a tactile perception. Medical researchers have known about synesthesia for three centuries, yet few of us have ever heard of this sense. Scientists believe that it is not just that certain people *have* this sense, but only that certain people have a malfunction in their filtering process that allows sense impressions generated by synaesthesia to become a part of conscious awareness. It is possible that everyone has this sense but most of us are just totally unaware of it. Further understanding of this sense may hold the key to consciousness and the relationship between reason and emotion, and at least shows that the human brain is even more mysterious and filled with unknown potentials than previously thought. [24]

So there is another sense after all - a seventh sense (counting proprioception as the sixth). How could synaesthesia be of benefit to the blind? Each sense is a channel through which we receive data about the world around us. This suggests that we may all be able to tap into other channels of information, other sources of data from which to create a better understanding.

---

[24] Recently knowledge of the workings of this sense has been made in language layman can follow through such books as, *The Man Who Tasted Shapes: A Bizarre Medical Mystery Offers Revolutionary Insights into Emotions, Reasoning, and Consciousness,* Richard E. Cytowic, Warner Books: New York, Abacus: London, 1993 © Richard E. Cytowic. *Synesthesia: A Union of the Senses,* Richard E. Cytowic, 01 June, 2002, published by MIT Press.

Training the Seventh Sense

It may be that certain types of phenomena, which have in the past been attributed to psychic powers, are really functions of the seventh sense. If so, then how do we train this sense?

If this sense operates according to the same principles as other senses, than by reducing the noise-to-signal ratio we should be able to increase the perception of synesthesia. The blind would indeed have a slight benefit in accessing this hidden sense since a large part of the sensory noise, vision, is gone. In the case of synaesthesia the noise one must reduce is that from all the other senses. Yet we come to a paradox, since we have spent much time in learning and expanding our sensory range how can we now discard that?

Perhaps it is not that one needs to reduce the noise of the other senses since they must form a part of the synesthesia process, but rather we must reduce the conclusions and expectations that the other senses create. This is how Zen differs from other forms of meditation. Rather than isolate the senses in order to focus on internal thoughts such as what occurs in an isolation tank, Zen teaches that it is not the senses that need to be suppressed but our expectations. 25

---

25 In a study that attracted much attention among meditation and biofeedback researchers during the 1960s, Akira Kasamatsu and Tomio Hirai, physicians at the University of Tokyo, studied the EEG changes exhibited during meditation by Zen teachers and their disciples (forty-eight in all) from Soto and Rinzai centers in Japan. For experimental control, they studied the EEGs of twenty-two

Our true understanding of the world is narrowed by filtering the information we do receive through learned patterns of perception. We know perception is an awareness of the environment through physical sensation, but not as well known is that these sensations are *interpreted* based on past experience. Experience creates certain precedents and expectations that change and filter our perception of the world.

---

subjects with no experience at meditation. They made EEG recordings; recorded their subjects' pulse rates, respiration, and galvanic skin response; and tested their responses to sensory stimuli during meditation. The Zen teachers and their most experienced students exhibited a typical progression of brain-wave activity during meditation, which Kasamatsu and Hirai divided into four stages:

- Stage 1: Characterized by the appearance of alpha waves in spite of opened eyes.
- Stage 2: Characterized by an increase in amplitude of persistent alpha waves.
- Stage 3: Characterized by a decrease in alpha frequency.
- Stage 4: Characterized by the appearance of rhythmical theta trains (Kasamatsu and Hirai, 1966).

Not all four stages were evident in every Zen practitioner, nor in any of the controls, but a strong correlation existed between the number of stages a given student exhibited and that student's length of time in Zen training. This correlation was supported by a Zen teacher's evaluation of each student's proficiency. The teacher ranked the students in three levels, without seeing their EEG records, and his rankings correlated well with Kasamatsu and Hirai's assessment of their EEGs.

The Kasamatsu-Hirai study also revealed significant differences between four Zen masters and four control subjects in their response to repetitive click stimuli. Like the Zen masters, the controls exhibited a blocking of alpha when a click sound first occurred, but they gradually became habituated to such stimuli so that their brain-wave activity no longer responded when a click was made. The Zen masters, however, did not become habituated, but continued to exhibit blocking as long as the stimuli continued. This finding indicates that Zen practice promotes a serene, alert awareness that is consistently responsive to both external and internal stimuli Kasamatsu, A., and T. Hirai. ": Science of Zazen." Psychologia 6 (1963): 86-91.

One way in which previous experience filters perception is known as *Inference*. Inference is the ability of the brain to automatically sort sensation into recognizable patterns. Perceptual inference operates by inferring the most likely possibility that can account for the sensory information available. This means that when the brain sorts through the data received by the senses it chooses the pattern which is the most familiar, even though that pattern may or may not accurately reflect the 'reality' of the external world.

For example, inference is the basis of the Rochart Ink Blot test whereby randomly created ink patterns are shown to a subject and they are asked to describe what they think the ink blots look like. Psychologists learn much about a person's personality based on the patient's interpretations. Another example would be if you were walking home in the dark after hearing a news report of a stalker in the area. You hear a sudden noise and turn quickly to see the silhouette of a man standing in the shadows. Upon investigation you see that it is only a bush or a shadow and that it was a cat or raccoon that made the noise. But initially you would have seen a man because of your expectation. If you had not heard the news report of the stalker, would you have seen a man or would you have seen a raccoon and some bushes?

Another factor in filtering perception is known as *Perceptual Set*. Perceptual set is the readiness to perceive stimulus in a particular way. Simply put; if you to expect to sense a particular sensation, then the sensory information you receive will be more likely interpreted according to your expectation. Past experience also contributes to your expectation creating a mind-set that will change the sensory information you receive into the expected sensation. For example, say someone held a lit cigarette near your hand and then asked you to close your eyes. If that person were to use a finger to touch your hand in the area where you had last seen the cigarette you would instinctively pull your hand away and for an instant believe you were burned. Your perceptual set was geared to interpret any sensation near the lit cigarette as heat.

Together these phenomena are known in psychology as the principle of Self Fulfilling Prophesy; which states that expectations influence perception and even tend to subconsciously direct a person's behaviour towards the fulfilment of that expectation. What all this means is that our previous life experience, and the expectations derived from them, combine to alter our views of the world.

A Zen Warrior is concerned about gathering real information about his or her environment, and not just information that will confirm his own preconceived notions. The blind also have preconceived ideas, such as what they are capable of doing and accomplishing, but are these ideas true? Or do commonly held expectations about the blind subtly alter, and in effect, sabotage their innate abilities?

The Zen technique for lessening the effects of expectation is known as detachment and is the first of three techniques used to try and tap into other ways of sensing.

An Archer, when practising in solitude, uses all of his skill, when shooting for the entertainment of house guests he uses three quarters of his skill, when shooting for a prize in a tournament he uses half his skill.
Japanese Proverb

Detachment

A person's ability to judge a signal correctly is affected by that person's response criterion. What the above quote illustrates is that the magnitude of the reward or punishment resulting from a correct judgement negatively affects your ability to make that judgement correctly. To paraphrase, the more nervous you are the more likely you are to make a mistake. This tendency to judge incorrectly when under pressure is why the ancient warriors practised detachment, win or lose, life or death, it was all the same because it had to be - if you cared, you died.

A Japanese story best illustrates the need for detachment. A government official who was of Samurai birth inadvertently insulted another hardened Samurai who demanded redress through a duel to be fought the next day. The official, because he was technically a Samurai, could not refuse but he had never even picked up a sword before and stood little chance of winning. In a last ditch effort he visited the city's most renowned sword master and told him of his predicament. The master replied "There is nothing I could teach you that would help in a sword fight but, being a government official you must practise the Tea Ceremony?"26

"Yes." replied the official, "I am very fond of the practise."

"Good!" said the master, "Tomorrow you should go and meet your death as though you were preparing tea. Thus you can achieve an honourable death befitting a Samurai." The next day the official went to the meeting place determined to die with honour, but when the other Samurai noticed the Official's calm demeanour he began to doubt; surely only the most experienced swordsman would come to a life or death duel with such nonchalance. Thinking better of the situation the other Samurai quickly apologized and called off the fight.

So how exactly do you practice detachment? Part of the answer is in desire. When we train, we desire certain results, when we focus on hearing or smell we desire to experience something new, when we practice self-defense techniques we desire our partner's defeat. While it is important to set and have measurable goals for a self-improvement program, it is during the actual practice itself that the

---

26 The Tea Ceremony (*Sado*) is a ritual way of preparing and drinking tea that is strongly influenced by Zen Buddhism. The ceremony itself consists of many small rituals that have to be learned by heart. Almost each hand movement, gesture and action is carefully prescribed. In a sense, the Tea ceremony is a form of *Kata* and requires the same focus and peace of mind.

desire for success can defeat the purpose. The writer Aldous Huxley in his little known book *The Art of Seeing* describes his experiences of having gone legally blind from a childhood illness 27 to restoring his vision through unusual, and some would say quack, eyeexercises. Echoing the Zen principle of detachment, he describes the biggest obstacle to seeing as the interference of the mind: *"Efforts on the part of the conscious "I" defeat their own objective. It is when you stop trying to see that seeing comes to you."*

The other part of the answer is the flip side of desire – aversion. Aversion to toil, aversion to failure, and aversion to suffering are just as detrimental as desire. So detachment can be said to be a calm non-emotional and non-judgmental observation. By cultivating an attitude of detachment one circumvents the mind's tendency to misinterpret information especially when under stress. This can apply to both the stress of everyday life and the stress of combat and survival.

We do not sit in meditation to someday become a Buddha,
when we sit in meditation, we are Buddha.
Shunryu Susuki, *Zen Mind, Beginner's Mind*

---

27 As a teenager, Aldous Huxley suffered an attack of keratitis punctata, an acute infection that left him with opacities in his cornea, farsightedness, and extreme blurriness. He was actually almost blind for 18 months. After that, his vision was still extremely poor; he was barely able to detect light with one eye, and only just barely able to see the largest letter on the Snellen (eye) chart at 10 feet.

Quiet & Isolation

Meditation or 'Internal' exercises like the Extended Hearing Exercise are most effective when conducted in quiet and isolation. The aim of these exercises is to focus and then catalogue certain sensory signals. To hear one's heartbeat, to feel postural tension, to flex individual muscles, to control the movements of the diaphragm, all require focusing on relatively weak sensory signals that are easily drowned out by the background noise of other sensations. This is why we instinctively hold our breath when working on delicate or complex tasks. (The sound and sensation of breathing can interfere with hand-to-eye coordination).

One reason to reduce external distraction is that the nervous system analyses stimulation in terms of sensory ratios, not in terms of absolute differences in sensory magnitude. This is known as Weber's Law and what it means is that the amount of stimulus necessary to produce a just noticeable difference is always a constant proportion of the overall intensity of the stimulus. For example, if you closed your eyes and I placed a one pound weight in your hand and then added another one pound weight you would notice the difference right away. The extra pound sends a signal that is 100% as strong as the original intensity, the first pound. But if I instead added a dime to the hand holding the one pound weight you would not notice the extra weight at all. The intensity of the signal caused by the weight of the dime is too small to overcome the overall signal intensity. That this phenomenon is a ratio can be demonstrated the same way. If instead of a one pound weight, I placed a feather in your hand you would feel the pressure of the feather against your skin. Now if I again placed a dime in the same hand you would notice right away the additional weight. A similar principle is in effect when we focus on any sensory perception. Often the signals we try to focus on are in a ratio too small to get through the generally high voltage sensory intensity that is our modern world. Taoist Tai Chi masters practise in parks and natural settings to promote calm and reduce the distracting noise of the outside world. Quiet and isolation are therefore necessary tools for practicing many of the exercises described in this program, and as a way of allowing other sensations to enter one's awareness.

Flow with whatever may happen and let your mind be free: stay centred by accepting whatever you are doing. This is the ultimate.
Chuang Tzu

Inner Calm

In addition to reducing outer sensory noise one must also learn to reduce inner sensory noise. This inner noise has two sources, emotions, and the internal dialogue.

The first form of calmness is emotional calm. Without going too deeply into complex subject of human emotions we need take note of only one characteristic, what could be called your brain's volume level. MRI scans show that "Feelings" create large sections of the brain to become active. This includes increased blood flow and transmission of electrochemical signals. Strong emotions create a high arousal level in the nervous system, in effect, turning up the volume. This loud noise is plugged into the mixing-board-like limbic system, that, in addition to processing sensory information, is also responsible for regulating emotions. To torture this metaphor further, we could say that calming one's feelings is like turning down the rest of the band so you can hear the singers. To reduce noise one must turn down the volume of emotional excitation. (Specific techniques to accomplish this will be discussed next chapter.)

Another internal source of noise is what has been called many things but is best described as internal dialogue - the almost non-stop conversation we have with ourselves. This endless internal rambling seems to be the product of the speech/vocalization area of the brain that just automatically produces dialogue much like a radio scanner randomly tuning into different radio programs. Like a radio scanner, the vocalization portion of the brain appears to scan through a dizzying array of weather reports, gossip, opinions, theories, asides, jokes and small talk and transmits all this largely useless information out onto the speaker system of our sensory cortex. Anyone having listened to someone who is drunk, has Turret's syndrome, or is vocalizing in a free association exercise can quickly discern that the brains seems to jump from subject to subject without any sense of rational purpose to it all. This happens even when we aren't vocalizing it. We basically all like the sound of our own voices, at least those that are in our heads.

Traditionally there have been two methods used to turn off the internal dialogue; recitation of *Mantras* (a few words or sounds repeated over and over), and counting breaths. Mantras seek to entrain the speech centre into a specific rhythm that prevents the dialogue from forming. This is done by repeating a single word or series of words that usually rhyme either out loud or internally.

Counting breaths is a just that, counting each breath you take from one to ten and then starting again at ten. This is a little more difficult since there are longer gaps of silence between counts (than with the constant rhythm of a Mantra) that allow the dialogue to creep in again. The act of *willing* the internal dialogue to stop is impossible to describe and seems to work only for brief periods of time. There are stories of Zen masters facing each other in a battle of minds whereby each stops the internal dialogue by sheer force of will. The loser being the one whose focus strays first. How it is done cannot be explained but like so much of what we have already learned, once you become aware of a new perception you already start to exert some control over it. When you are in a situation that requires acute perception you must silence the inner noise.

So what is there then when we stop the noise, and cease fretting? What sensations are there then to perceive and what benefit can be derived from it all? Well there are two answers neither of which is very satisfying.

First, any answer found would be inexplicable. *"If you can tell me what the Tao is, it is not the Tao."* says Lao Tzu one of the founders of Taoism. This is not really as profound as it might sound coming from such an ancient sage. Many, if not most, things are inexplicable such as the taste of chocolate or the color purple. Verbalize all you like but you cannot explain them to someone who has not experienced them. So there may be something more to the human experience but you could never tell anyone about it.

Second, whatever benefits derived are likewise too subtle to perceive clearly. It's more like becoming luckier. To say you become smarter or more skilful would be to overstate the case. The changes are almost too small to notice, but like a pebble that starts an avalanche the overall impact on your life may be much more profound.

Chapter 5

Fear

The warrior is never amazed. If somebody comes up to you and says "I'm going to kill you right now" or "I have a present of a million dollars for you," you are not amazed. You simply assume your seat on the saddle.

Chogyam Trungpa, *Shambala, The Sacred Path of The Warrior*.

One of the most common fears is fear of the dark. Who hasn't felt frightened of being in the dark at some point during childhood? Perhaps it was during your first summer camp walking to the outhouse alone in the dark near the woods? Or possibly you felt it stumbling through the darkened hallway of your home during a power blackout? One explanation is that this is an instinctive fear of nocturnal predators, one that allowed our ancient ancestors to survive by huddling in terrified groups on the primordial savannahs of Africa. Another theory is that fear of the dark is a form of xenophobia - the fear of the unknown and is perhaps the basis of all fears. Fear of the dark is a fear of not knowing what's out there. And the reason we don't know what's out there is because we are deprived of our most important warning system, vision.

Like most of us, Susan had several fears. There are the emotional fears of being alone, of being unwanted, of being a burden. She also had practical fears such as fear of fires and strangers, yet fear itself is not always the problem, actually we need to be afraid sometimes. Fear is nature's guardian that warns and alerts the organism to real or perceived dangers. To understand the role that fear plays in human survival it is interesting to see the effects of people who have lost the ability to be afraid. An extremely rare condition, known as Urbok Vita disease, destroys the amygdala, that part of the brain that is responsible for fear. Victims of this disease literally do not know the meaning of the word fear. They cannot make facial expressions of fear nor do they recognize expressions of fear in others. Most revealing however is that victims of this disease have lost the ability to sense danger. Because of this lack of a sense of danger, they have a short life expectancy. Most patients die young due to accidents that fear, had they felt it, would have warned them to avoid. Fear is thus a survival instinct. It is only when we have too much or an irrational fear that it becomes a drawback.

Knowledge of fear provides important lessons for those who practise the way of the warrior. Fear is a natural component of combat but also there is a certain bravery required to learn to overcome one's own handicaps. For Susan some of the exercises we introduced caused a degree of fear. We had to deal with fear early on in our training, but before we could learn to control fear we need to know what it does. Let's begin with what we know about fear and its effects on the body.

The Physiological Basis of Fear

Fear is a reflex startle response triggered through perception. Humans are genetically programmed to fear certain types of situations such as strangers, large objects, unknown sounds, or anything rushing towards you. These are known as primary fears and are a part of our survival instinct. However, primary fears can create secondary fears that are less a part of survival, and more a creation of imagination. For example, the basic fear of strangers can be expanded to include fear of strange fashions, hairstyles, languages, the fear of crowds, and even such intangibles as fear of new ideas or conflicting opinions - all can induce feelings ranging from anxiety to terror.

The perception of a threat causes a reaction in the autonomic nervous system whose job it is to prepare the human organism for sudden and frantic activity. This is known as the `Fight or Flight' response. [28] This reaction acts as a survival mechanism preparing the body to either flee a potential predator through the hazards of open terrain in a race to the death, or to make a final stand in a life or death struggle. Either way the body must be able to call on every ounce of energy and numb any pain that might interfere with fighting or running.

---

28. First noted by physiologist Walter Cannon in the 1920s. *The Mind,* Richard M. Restak, Bantam Books, New York, 1988.

The autonomic nervous system is made up of the sympathetic and the parasympathetic nervous systems that are responsible for preparing the body for action and preserving strength respectively. In the initial stages of fear, the sympathetic nervous system triggers the endocrine system to release hormones causing the following symptoms:

- Increased heart rate to increase the flow of blood throughout the body
- Respiration is affected either by hyperventilating or holding in the breath
- Arteries are dilated to increase blood flow to the surface to provide the anticipated demand of oxygen from the muscles. (This can be recognized by the face becoming red as the blood is sent out to the external muscles)
- Body temperature increases producing sweat, and body hair may become erect
- Blood flow to the digestive organs is restricted to provide more blood to the muscles, the stomach may suddenly feel nauseous, and vomiting may occur

In addition, the pituitary gland releases a hormone to stimulate the adrenals which in turn increases the availability of blood sugar (glucose) and increases the body's ability to release stored energy. This process is akin to revving the engine and feeding nitrous oxide into a fuel mixture. Endorphins, whose molecular structure closely resembles morphine, are also released into the brain to numb the anticipated pain of injuries and fatigue.

However, the body cannot maintain this heightened state of readiness for long. Soon the parasympathetic system is triggered into action to counter the effects of the sympathetic system. The parasympathetic system tries to reverse all the changes caused by the sympathetic system: Heart rate is reduced, breathing becomes shallow, gasping, with frequent sighing, and the mouth becomes dry. Blood is drawn in towards the inner body restricting the flow to the brain, which may cause dizziness, seeing spots in the peripheral vision, and fainting. The face becomes pale and waxy, body temperature is lowered. The digestive system may suddenly kick in causing a sudden bowel movement or release of the bladder. For a short period the two systems alternate back and forth in a battle for control of the body's nervous system, a battle always won in the end by the parasympathetic. All these opposing responses can take place in a matter of minutes. During actual fighting or fleeing the available stores of energy is burned off through frenetic activity. So how does this knowledge of fear benefit us in a practical way? Well there are a couple things.

Knowledge of how fear affects the body is the basis for a very effective combat strategy that both Sun Tzu and Miyamoto Musashi wrote about called the 'Await the Enemy at Your Ease' and the 'Delayed Attack' strategies. This is how it works. At the start of any battle, either between large forces or between individuals, both sides will start out in a high state of readiness. Fear is a major factor and in the early stages triggers the sympathetic system to insure that fighters are in the prime physiological condition to fight. The Delayed Attack Strategy requires that you stall the opponent from attacking. Through distraction or retreat you cause the opponent to use up his available time in a hyper ready state. Within 5 to 15 minutes the parasympathetic system takes over and there is little one can do to stop the nervous system from gearing down. While you stall and wait out your opponent, you must also be able to control your own level of excitation so that you do not likewise peak too soon. Once the opponent's spirit for the fight has been deflated, you attack. This catches the opponent in a depressed state which provides you with a tremendous advantage. In a street fight, robbery, mugging, or in an attempted rape situation it is important to time your counter-attack to take advantage of this principle.

But this information can be useful in interpersonal situations as well. Anger, like fear, will stimulate the same sympathetic and parasympathetic responses. When confronted with an angry person a sighted person would first notice the effects of the sympathetic response in the redness of the person's face, their bulging eyes, and jerky body language. For the blind there are other, non-visual clues to tell you about the anger and fear dynamics of someone close to you. The first clue would come from listening to the person's breathing patterns. Rapid heavy breathing would mean a person is pumping adrenalin and oxygen and would indicate the most volatile stage in the cycle. You should also listen to the sounds of what is called displacement activity. An angry person will need to dissipate the energy caused by the heightened state of readiness and they often do so by short fast violent actions such as stomping the ground, slamming a fist onto a table top, or slamming a door. When an angry person is winding down you should hear an increase in sighing sometimes interspersed with hyperventilating. You may also hear the person's movements become sluggish almost drunken. The muscles, having failed to use up the increase in glucose, starts to poison itself with lactic acid which causes the muscles to tremble, feel weak, and even cramp.

Fear and anger causes tension which means muscles become tighter. The larynx is also a muscle and as it tightens up from stress you can hear that both the person's volume level and pitch will rise - another clue that the person is in an excited state. As anger subsides the muscles of the larynx like the other muscles may begin to tremble and you will begin to hear a cracking and trembling quality to the voice.

In the initial stage of anger and fear the body temperature will increase and cause perspiration. We know that perspiration is saturated with human hormones and these hormones would reflect the high adrenalin chemical state of the body. This is what animals smell when they sense that a person is afraid of them. It may even be conceivable that you could learn to recognize the smell of fear/anger.

The strategy for dealing with an enraged person is thus the same as the Delayed Attack strategy. At first you delay and stall and wait for the anger to dissipate. This is not the time to react with anger or to start an argument. Instead listen, say little, and agree to some points. Once the peak stage of anger and excitement is over you can gently begin to control the situation. Have the person sit down, go home, or relax. After a while you can try reasoning with the person. By using this strategy you can avoid potential violence.

Thus far fear has taught us a ruthless strategy to use in confrontations, and how to read and react to an angry person in an interpersonal situation. But the most important thing fear has to teach us is how to tame it.

Taming Fear

Courage is resistance to fear, mastery of fear, not absence of fear.
Mark Twain

As we have learned fear is used to prepare the body for combat. The accompanying increase in strength, pain threshold, and endurance can be lifesaving assets. It is not something we want to do without. However, too often fear turns to panic and it is then that fear becomes a liability. Panic blinds us to the nature of the threat and prevents us from seeing other options. In hand-to-hand combat, panic will reduce a fight to a mindless struggle. A cunning fighter searches for weakness, advantages, opportunities, and weapons, the tools that allow the weak to overcome the strong. Our ancestors were no match physically for any but the smallest predators yet we stand at the top of the food chain for no other reason that we are a cunning, and perhaps even a diabolical, species. The blind are physically at a disadvantage against many of society's modern predators but using the same tools our species used to survive they can improve the odds considerably. But cunning requires an awareness of mind. The problem exists not in erasing fear entirely from our minds, even if it were possible, but rather a delicate balance of enhanced awareness and body readiness, combined with a detached self-control.

The basic technique in fear control involves countering the actions of the sympathetic and parasympathetic responses. For example, when the sympathetic system urges hyperventilation, we consciously slow our breathing. When the parasympathetic system urges shallow breathing, we consciously breathe deeper. Where tension arises, we relax, and when we feel tired, we tense. Let's see how breathing and relaxation are used to tame fear.

Breathing

The diaphragm is usually controlled unconsciously by the autonomous nervous, but can also come under the control of our conscious volition. This wiring provides and avenue through which the mind can influence several unconscious functions such as heart rate, muscle tension, blood pressure, and brain wave pattern. It is for this reason that breathing techniques lie at the heart of most Yogic and *Chi Kung* 29 exercises. Breathing control is also the primary means to tame the 'Fight or Flight' response.

So when you practice Zazen, your mind should be concentrated on your breathing. This kind of activity is the fundamental activity of the universal being. Without this experience, this practice, it is impossible to attain absolute freedom.

Shunryu Suzuki, *Zen Mind, Beginner's Mind.*

The nervous system's first reaction to powerful and painful stimulus is to reduce system noise by reducing or suspending breathing. The perception of a threat triggers an instinct to make as little noise as possible and to concentrate all the senses on the source of the stimulus. Holding the breath reduces some of the sensory background noise made by the respiratory system enabling us to focus more intensely. We still have this instinct. Whenever we concentrate our attention, try to listen carefully, or to see something that is not too clear, we tend to either hold our breath or breathe shallowly. However, if the stimulus is particularly strong the shutting down mechanism may be overridden and the person

---

29 *Chi Kung* is a Chinese term that means "Life-Energy Technique" and refers to a series of breathing and mental exercises that are aimed at improving strength, health, and longevity.

will spontaneously hyperventilate. Holding the breath for too long while the sympathetic nervous system is stimulated into high gear causes a sudden demand for oxygen, the signal to breathe is somehow overstated and, instead of rhythmical deep breathing, the person will begin to hyper-ventilate.

During hyperventilation, a greater than average amount of carbon dioxide is washed out of the bloodstream. The body needs a certain amount of CO_2 and a rapid drop of CO_2 will constrict blood flow to many vital organs resulting in diverse and sometimes serious symptoms. Constriction of blood vessels in the brain will cause dizziness, disorientation, and may lead to loss of consciousness. A similar occurrence in the heart may lead to chest pains. The high oxygen level also creates greater amounts of alkaline that can make one nervous and edgy, and cause a feeling of `pins and needles', muscle spasms, nervous twitches, and even convulsions. An old home remedy to treat hyperventilation is to breath into a paper bag. Since we breathe out more carbon dioxide than oxygen, the air in the paper bag, after a couple of breaths, will contain more CO_2 which in turn will be inhaled back into the lungs and help balance the oxygen/CO_2 levels to return breathing to normal. But we can accomplish the same effect through controlled breathing techniques.

Calming Breath

The first step to correcting hyperventilation is to realize that you are doing it. Simply being aware of this reaction will help to overcome its effects. Remember to breathe deep and rhythmically anytime you feel threatened or anxious. Focus on your abdomen and take three short breaths holding each for one second before exhaling. On the fourth breath begin deep breathing at a medium tempo.

Abdominal or Deep Breathing

This type of breathing technique is best done in conjunction with some other exercises in this program such as the `Holding the Jug' and `Extended Hearing' exercises. When practising 'Internal' exercises, we need slow rhythmic breathing that aids in the production of beta and theta brainwave patterns associated with relaxation, visualization, and recovery. Abdominal breathing mimics the natural breathing that occurs during the stage of sleep know as REM (Rapid Eye Movement). It is during REM sleep that we dream and it is thought that during this stage that the conscious and sub-conscious minds share information.

Directions:

1. Begin with the three short rapid breaths, and then draw in the air through the nose and into the lower abdomen as though inflating a balloon in the belly.

2. Inhale slowly up to a count of ten, then hold the breath in for a count of three, and then exhale again up to a count of ten. Be sure that the length of inhalation is equal to the exhalation.

Since we know that anger can cause the same responses as fear, the above two breathing techniques are also useful to practise should you become angry yourself.

In the chapter on the Seventh Sense we learned how important it is to remain calm while training. The type of training outlined in this manual is complex and sometimes painful. It is natural to occasionally feel frustrated and angry. It is at these times too that you can use breathing techniques to calm down, overcome the pain and frustration, and continue training.

Abdominal breathing is a useful tool to help you remain calm and relaxed during a tense situation and to reduce feelings of fear. Since we are on the topic of breathing there are two other breathing techniques that are of benefit to martial artists - rhythmic breathing and bamboo breathing.

Rhythmic Breathing

During the practise of martial arts techniques it is important to exhale when executing a technique, and to inhale during the retraction or pause between techniques. For example, when executing a punch you exhale when punching out, and inhale when retracting the hand back to its guard position. This is true for other forms of exercise as well. When doing push-ups you exhale when pushing off the ground (exertion) and inhale when dropping back down (relaxation). In weight training you exhale during the lift or contraction, and inhale during the release and return.

Rhythmic breathing is useful for repetitive exercises such as callisthenics, aerobics, running, and of course martial arts. These activities follow a tempo that can be linked to a breathing rhythm. For example, long distance runners know to regulate their breathing with the tempo of their footsteps. A four/four rhythm would mean that the inhalation would take as long as it does to run four steps, and the exhalation also would take four steps to complete. Proper rhythm can also have a hypnotizing effect. Marathon runners commonly report that they enter into a trance-like state in which they are no longer aware of pain and exhaustion. When breathing and movement are out of tempo it hinders coordination and loses economy of motion and thus energy. As a rule, when moving remember to match your breathing rhythm to the tempo of your actions and follow the general rule that when you exert effort you should breath out. This will enhance both the ability to breath and the ability to move efficiently.

Bamboo Breathing

While rhythmic breathing is used for medium speed movements, rapid combinations of movements such as speed drills, and during actual combat, do not allow enough time between each action to inhale. This would require that you either inhale during times of exertion, or hold your breath during several movements until there is pause to breathe again. Either method would compromise power and leave you susceptible to exhaustion and even possible injury. For example, let's say you are practicing a jab and reverse punch combination (in boxing known as the old 'One-Two' punch). The timing of these two actions is very close together, a 'one-two' rhythm, there is no time between the 'one' and the 'two' in which to draw in another breath and exhale in time for the second punch. How then do you insure that you are breathing out during both actions? The answer to this is what is known as Bamboo Breathing.[30]

Bamboo Breathing gets its name from the way in which Chinese and Japanese painters draw bamboo using the traditional brush and ink. This is accomplished by drawing a smooth line, then stopping the stroke for a short pause, lifting the brush from the paper, then continuing the stroke repeating the pause and lift until the bamboo stalk is finished. The pauses allow more ink to be absorbed into the paper thickening the stalk slightly, and the lift leaves a narrow empty space between each segment which creates the bamboo's signature joint pattern. Bamboo breathing follows the same method. The breath is drawn in and then exhaled in a short puff of air at the exact moment of exertion, then paused, then exhaled again and so on. In this way you can execute several techniques in rapid succession by taking in one breath and then exhaling short powerful puffs of air with each technique until the lungs are emptied. No more than three or four techniques should be done with one breath, and then you must pause or retreat to gain another breath.

---

30. From Hewit, James, *Meditation*, Teach Yourself Books, G.B. 1978, Quote from Katsuki Sekidas' *Zen Training*.

Another way to insure that you are breathing out during the execution of a technique is to use vocalizations. While the Japanese *Kiai* or `spirit yell' is often used with the finishing blow, it is impractical when executing multiple and rapid attacks. Instead, use short exhalations accompanied by a guttural sound that ends in a sharp cut-off of air. Sounds such as 'Hup' or 'Hut', help coordinate exhalations to movement. This is one of the reasons some styles incorporate animal sounds into their combat training. The vocalizations help insure that you are exhaling when exerting force.

Relaxation

There are two types of relaxation: passive and dynamic. Passive relaxation is where the body rests and is in a state of repose, dynamic relaxation is the state of the body and mind that is associated with normal and natural functioning. Malfunctioning and strain tend to appear whenever the conscious "I" interferes with instinctively acquired habits of proper use.
Aldous Huxley, *The Art of Seeing*

Tension is a semi-aroused state that stimulates the sympathetic and parasympathetic nervous systems simultaneously. In engineering terms this is like revving the throttle and applying the brakes at the same time - eventually the machine breaks down. Fear and anxiety are the natural sources of tension and so another method to reduce fear is to exert some degree of control over tension.

Chronic tension is also a destructive habit that almost everyone develops to some degree. It is the source of innumerable illnesses and diseases and interferes with almost every aspect of human functioning.[31] Learning to control tension not only aids in reducing fear and anxiety but also provides numerous other benefits such as lowered blood pressure, more restful sleep, better digestion, more energy, and greater freedom of motion to name a few. In the art of war, unconscious tension is a hindrance, the equivalent of carrying around unnecessary baggage.

Controlling Tension

Tension is insidious, in the beginning it is easy to recognize tense muscle groups and to relax them using the techniques described here but, the problem occurs the minute one's attention is distracted, then old habits return and tension slowly takes over the body again. The only way to prevent this is to develop new habits over a long period of time. Breaking old habits and forming new ones requires that you consciously intervene before the expression of those behaviours you wish to change. In the case of unconscious tension, one must learn to consciously focus on relaxation at precisely those

---

31. Tension or more correctly hyper tension has been linked to increases in the incidence of numerous human ailments such as heart attack, stroke, high blood pressure, cancer, headache, vision problems, as well as psychological dysfunctions such as anxiety, depression, hyper-activity, and learning disorders.

Furthermore, in the tradition of Chinese acupuncture tension is seen as the cause for numerous ailments (as it is in western tradition with the theory of A personality types being more susceptible to heart attacks). According to Chi Gung theory tension impedes the flow of Chi, The area that is thus tensed becomes weakened and disease soon follows.

times when one is most inclined to become tense. The paradox is that at these times relaxation is usually the last thing one wants to think about. This effect can be seen in job interviews, presentations, public speaking, meeting new people, and the endless daily confrontations and disputes we have with our fellow man. At each encounter one's attention is trapped by the external circumstances and the overall degree of tension rises a little more. However, once you learn and have practised the following relaxation techniques it will only take you a few moments to relax completely and you can do this quickly anytime you feel tense.

The following exercises all require a quiet place free from interruption, that you wear relaxed loose clothing, and that you sit in a comfortable sitting or reclining position, and use slow rhythmic breathing.

Classical Conditioning

One of the most effective methods for reducing tension is through Behavioural Conditioning techniques. Behavioural conditioning originated with Ivan Pavlov and his famous experiments with dogs. Pavlov would ring a bell each time he fed the dogs. After a while, the dogs would salivate when they heard the bell even when there was no food placed before them. He discovered that if you start with a stimulus and response that are already connected with each other (food and salivation), then add a third stimulus (bell), eventually the third stimulus becomes so strongly associated with the original stimulus that it has the power to produce the original behavior response(salivation).

This principle forms the basis of various behavioural conditioning techniques whereby one purposely pairs certain types of stimulus with a certain desired response. The following program will connect a word/image with relaxation exercises so that, after repeated efforts, you will be able to instantly relax merely by mentally repeating a word to yourself.

Choose any word or phrase that evokes a feeling of peace and relaxation such as "Cool Moss", "Warm Fire", or "Summer Breeze". This word/image will serve as the (conditioned) stimulus. The next step is to build a memory picture around the phrase that will improve the relaxation response. This is done by associating the phrase with as many relaxing sensory memories as possible to add emotional energy. For example, take the phrase "Summer Breeze" and build a memory picture by visualizing the glow of the sunset over the ocean, and the scenery in pastel pinks, peaches, and gold. Smell the salty spray from the ocean, mixed with the scent of coconut oil and fried bananas. Feel the warm sensation of the sun on your face and the breeze in your hair, the sand under your feet. Imagine hearing the steady rhythm of the surf and the cries of sea birds. Each individual sense has its own relaxation response trigger built in. The feeling of warmth, the sound of a waterfall, the smell of home baked bread, each can trigger the body to relax. Using them in combination increases the effectiveness of this technique. Once the word stimulus and memory picture have been created in your imagination, the next step is to condition the response through consciously directed relaxation methods.

Releasing the Bowstring

This exercise requires that you first tense your body as much as possible and then to suddenly release all the tension at once. The tensing of the body is like drawing the string of a bow, and then releasing the tension is like releasing the string of the bow. This is best done lying on your back, before going to sleep, but can also be done sitting up or even standing. First, tense every major muscle in the body starting at the feet and quickly moving up the legs, thighs, buttocks, stomach, chest, shoulders, arms, fingers, and finally, hold the mouth and eyes wide open. (Yes this is better practiced in private as you will look a quite ridiculous.)

Maintain this tension for a count of five, then repeat mentally to yourself the previously chosen word/image and immediately relax the entire body at once as though you were dropping a great weight. The body acts like the bow when being drawn, becoming tense with potential energy. Triggering the relaxation response is like releasing the arrow; all tension in the bow immediately dissipates.

Perform this exercise three times just before going to sleep each evening. In a few days you will be able to repeat the word/image to yourself under everyday conditions and immediately feel the release of tension you were previously unaware of.

Systematic Muscle Relaxation

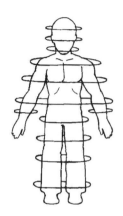

In this method one consciously relaxes specific muscle groups in sequential order while mentally repeating the word/image. Begin this exercise from the top. First, direct your attention to your face and sense your facial expression. Are you frowning or are the eyebrows raised in wonderment? Are you grimacing or smiling? Consciously isolate and relax the muscles around the eyes and mouth, over the forehead and around the jaw. Imagine them relaxing and releasing their tension while mentally repeating the word/image. Then work down the body isolating and relaxing specific muscle groups. The general sequence is as follows.

Head: Forehead, eyes, mouth, jaw, back of the head, neck.

Torso: Trapezes and shoulder muscles, the chest, abdomen, back along the spine, lumbar, buttocks.

Limbs: The arms starting with the shoulders and working towards the hands and ending in the finger tips, thighs, calves, and feet.

Some people may have difficulty *willing* their muscles to relax, since the effort to relax often defeats its own purpose. In such cases there are two other strategies that can be used. The first method attempts to circumvent the effort/tension response by working on an unconscious level. As one systematically isolates each muscle group, do not make any effort to relax; instead one imagines feeling warmth flowing into the muscle. The heat metaphor promotes blood circulation to the muscle and aids relaxation.[32] Another approach is to first tense each muscle group in order to better isolate the kinaesthetic sense of each muscle. In biofeedback terms this is known as increasing the `Signal to Noise Ratio'. To focus on a specific stimulus you must increase its signal in order to recognize it above the sensory background noise. To increase a muscle's sensation, first tense the muscle for a few seconds which makes it easier to focus upon. This signal is then used to send back a relaxation response by simply un-tensing the muscle. With practise you will be able to recognize each muscle group's state of tension and develop a better 'feel' for your body's musculature.

Systematic De-sensitization

As with the breathing exercises, the relaxation exercises can also be used to control anger and to remain calm during emergencies. Although the above breathing and relaxation methods are effective

---

32. Dr. Johann Shultz and Wolfgang Luthe devised relaxation techniques called *Autogenic* training that focused on six standard exercises to create at will the sensations of heaviness, warmth, actual reduction of the heart rate, change in respiration, apparent warming of the solar plexus, and cooling of the forehead. John B. Alexander, *The Warrior's Edge.*

in controlling the feeling of fear we also need a way to overcome specific fears and phobias. Fortunately there is a simple yet effect technique to help overcome specific fears.

Systematic de-sensitization is a process by which an immunity to fear is built up through small doses of fear taken under controlled conditions.[33] The following example will provide the framework from which a similar de-sensitization program can be created.

First, one must isolate and deal with one fear at a time, then go through a list of possible scenarios that would be considered frightening and rate each scenario on a scale from one to ten in degree of fear invoked. For example, if you are afraid of heights, then the scenario of standing on a chair may rate a 1 on the scale of fear. Standing on the second rung of a latter may be rated a 4, while climbing a tree rates an 8. Various scenarios are imagined, rated on the scale from one to ten and noted. This list will provide the progression for your conditioning program. Begin with activities rated on the scale of one, such as standing on a chair. First, go through the basic relaxation and calming breath routines while seated in a quiet room. Once you feel relaxed, begin to imagine climbing up and standing on the chair. If at any time during the visualization you start to feel tense or afraid, stop and return to the

33. Behaviorists use Systemic Desensitization, credited to Joseph Wolpe. This method gradually introduces visualizations of disturbing stimuli while the subject is relaxed, so that objects and situations they represent become less threatening.

relaxation exercises. This process is repeated until you can visualize the scenario without any anxiety or tension. Once this stage is completed, the next phase recreates the scenario with an actual chair. As with the visualization you relax and then approach the chair. Again if you detect any tension return to your seat and relax. Repeat the above until you are able to stand up on the chair without any fear. Next, work on those scenarios that rated 2 on the scale of fear using the same procedure starting with the relaxation and visualization exercises, and then moving to actual recreation. The same process works for as far up the scale as seems necessary. Naturally it is not necessary to balance on top of a flagpole to overcome the fear of climbing a ladder, or sit in a box of pit vipers to overcome the fear of snakes.

With Susan we identified four fears: fear of weakness and fainting (Asthenophobia), fear of a fire in the house, fear of open spaces or of being in crowded public places (Agoraphobia) and fear of being a victim of sexual assault (Agra phobia). It was the last fear that had motivated Susan to seek self-defense lessons. Each was different and each required a slightly different approach, but all were easily overcome using a combination of the above techniques.

The first fear we encountered during training was the fear of weakness and fainting. Susan was sure that if left alone outdoors her legs would buckle from a feeling of weakness in her legs. As we have seen in chapter one, the solution to this fear was grounding and balance training. This training incorporated all of the above fear reduction techniques. In the first few weeks of the stance and grounding training I would stand close to Susan to reassure her that, should she feel faint, I would be there to catch her. Meantime she used the breathing exercises to help her relax and focus on her balance. Gradually I would step further away from Susan until she could practise on her own without the need for a 'spotter'. In this way, we worked to de-sensitize her from the fear of standing alone, by gradually increasing the difficulty and isolation. As her leg strength and balance improved so did her confidence until after a couple of months this fear was completely absent in her life.

We devised a simple procedure for overcoming the worry of a potential fire in the house. We wrote out a checklist to follow before leaving the house and before going to sleep at night. Susan would first go to the kitchen and check the stove settings to insure they were off. Then she checked the appliances such as the toaster and microwave. Then she would methodically go into every room in the house and sniff. By this time, we had gone through the tracking exercise and it gave Susan confidence in her ability to smell fire so that a good whiff in each room would reassure her that there was nothing smoldering.

Overcoming Susan's fear of traveling alone took only a little longer. Again, we used the desensitizing method. We began with breathing and relaxation exercises followed by short walks to the end of the block and back in which I accompanied her. After a few trials

Susan could walk go the end of the block and back alone using her white cane to feel along the sidewalk while I watched in case she should become disoriented and panic. We slowly increased the difficulty level. The first few times the journey would be made with my accompaniment and then Susan would go solo. In this way Susan became acclimatized to walking around the block, then to walking to the corner store and back, and finally to go into town on her own.

The last fear we tackled was the fear of being attacked and helpless to fight back. Actually none of the above techniques were used at all for this. This was not an unwarranted fear and to ignore such a possibility would only make a person more vulnerable to attack. As we learned at the beginning of this chapter fear is a survival instinct. Susan's survival instinct told her she was vulnerable and in fact she was vulnerable. She sought out self-defence training as a response to her instinctive fear thus increasing her chances of survival. This is exactly why nature gave us fear. Once Susan learned that she had the ability to defend herself, her confidence increased. As her confidence increased, the less afraid she became.

Walking Lesson

All of the pervious walking lessons also served to reduce fear. By describing and recognizing sounds and smells, the unknown was made known. The more a student learns about his or her environment, the less afraid they will be. As you continue with the walking lessons keep this in mind. Whenever something unusual or out of place occurs during the walk explain what happened. By providing descriptions of events your student will be better able recognize the sounds and smell of odd events thus increasing their repertoire of sound identifications and knowledge of their surroundings. All of which will also help to reduce anxiety and fear.

Thus far we have dealt with almost every other subject except for the one which Susan initially called me for, to learn self-defence. Yet this is a natural progression for all martial artists not just those with vision impairment. We all must first learn to be grounded and solid, to learn how to be balanced and move gracefully, to focus and pay attention to details, and to relax and overcome fears. Most martial arts instructors are familiar with all of the above subjects and would find little difficulty in adapting their teaching methods to accommodate visually impaired students as well. Now we will turn to the nuts and bolts of martial arts, the self-defence techniques.

Chapter 6

Self-Defence

It is a doctrine of war not to assume the enemy will not come, but rather to rely on one's readiness to meet him; not to presume that he will not attack, but rather to make one's self invincible.

Sun Tzu, *The Art of War*

There are hundreds of martial arts styles worldwide and they vary widely in their approach to hand-to-hand combat. One approach that divides them is the difference between Strike systems and Grappling systems. The strike-oriented styles focus on using the hands and feet to strike an attacker, while grappling styles focus on grabbing and throwing an attacker. Most martial arts combine elements from both systems with only a few being devoted exclusively to just one approach. Boxing, for example, is purely a strike system with no grabbing or throwing allowed while Sumo is purely a grappling system with no striking or hitting allowed.

In deciding which techniques were best suited to Susan's needs, I chose to emphasize the grappling system. While punches and kicks look impressive and are usually the techniques seen in action movies, the drawback is that they are not very practical for self-defense unless you have studied for quite some time. In Susan's situation, she could not afford the time and resources to pursue this type of long-term training. Another reason is that with striking techniques there is a distinct advantage if you can see what you are aiming a punch at. With a grappling technique, you start by being in contact with your opponent and with some practice, a blind person could be just as adept as a sighted person could in feeling the opponent's moves and countering. This makes sense in that to sexually or physically assault someone the attacker would by necessity have to come into close contact with the intended victim. Once in physical contact, a blind person can sense the attacker's position and counter attack. And because the attacker is in close range, grappling techniques are the most practical. Therefore, the following self-defence techniques focus mostly on grappling techniques with only a few strikes thrown in for good measure.

Touch Sensitivity

"Master how is it that even though you are blind, you know there is a grasshopper at my feet?" asked young Cain.
"It would be better to ask how, even though you can see,
you did not know there is grasshopper at your feet." replied
master Po.
Dialogue from *Kung Fu*

In order to defend against an attacker, a blind student would need to create a reasonably accurate mental image of the attacker's physical location and position. This is not as difficult as may initially seem. There are a limited number of ways in which one person can attack another. By rehearsing those attacks a blind student can learn to recognize each attack and the accompanying body position an attacker would assume in order to attack in that manner. Once you know the attacker's position, you can counterattack. For example, if an attacker was to place you in a side headlock and his body was on your left side, then you would know three things. One, that the attacker is using his right arm, two, that the attacker's right leg would be positioned to the front of your left leg. Three, you would then know the position of the attacker's testicles, and have a fair chance of accurately grabbing them - a painful and effective defence against a side headlock.

To train Susan to recognize attack patterns and to improve her sense of touch we began with simple grabs, done lightly and slowly. I would reach out and grab her wrist and ask her to just guess which hand I was using. We discovered that the biggest clue was to feel for the pressure exerted by the thumb. Once she was able to accurately identify which hand I was using, the next step was to extrapolate on that information and make a guess as to where I was standing relative to her. For example, when I am using my right hand to grab her left wrist, am I standing behind, to the side, or in front of her? In addition to using information derived from the actual grab, the other senses are also needed to determine the attacker's position. Using the senses of smell, heat, and auditory occlusion, Susan quickly became adept at sensing my body position. The next step was to learn how to counter attack. For example, if I grabbed Susan by the throat she learned to sense my position and then counter attack using either a hand strike to a pressure point or a kick to the legs. These are first response techniques used to distract the attacker. Finally, we worked on the escapes and counter techniques.

The following training drills help students to create a mental image of the position another person would assume in order to execute some of the most common types of attacks.

Touch Sensitivity Exercise

In this exercise, the student stands in a cleared area and remains still as the trainer walks around the student stopping every few seconds to grab the student with one hand. Once the trainer grabs hold, the student is told to focus on the *feeling* that grab creates and to guess whether it is the trainer's right or left hand. The trainer corrects any wrong guesses. Initially the trainer should grip the student firmly starting with the wrist and arm and then progressing to shoulders and neck. Warning: Never use force in grabbing the throat. Instead, very gently place your hand in the choke position but without exerting any pressure.

By using a firm grip, the subject is better able to feel the placement of the thumb, by knowing the thumb placement one can deduce which hand is gripping.

For the next stage, once the grab has been made, the trainer remains silent and waits for the student to place his or her hand on the trainer's chest bone. In the beginning, the student should use the free hand to feel along the arm the trainer is using to grab with, and along the shoulders and chest to create and confirm a mental image of the trainer's position. As training progresses, the student should then be able to place his or her hand accurately on the trainer's chest without needing to feel along the arm.

The final stage is a little dangerous and the trainer needs to wear a face shield and/or hold a focus pad in front of his face to act as a target. At this stage, the student learns to strike the trainer's throat and nose using open hand techniques. This is similar to the previous exercise except that instead of touching the center of the trainer's chest, the student learns to strike the throat, neck, and nose. These are the most vulnerable targets accessible to a defender so training to hit these targets is the best reaction to a sudden attack. In the beginning have the student execute the techniques in slow motion and gently touch the targets.

When the student is able to touch these targets accurately the trainer then puts on the protective equipment and holds the focus pad in front of his face. First, have the student practice a few dozen back knife-hand strikes to the throat and neck targets gradually increasing the speed and force of the strikes. Then the practice the heel palm strike to the nose.

Back Knife Hand Strike

This strike aimed at the neck or throat. Let us break this technique down. If the attacker grabs your left hand, you use your right hand to counter attack thus. First, bring your right hand across your chest palm down as though you were to pat yourself on your left shoulder. Flatten your hand and keep the fingers slightly curled and held tight together.

1.   2.

Extend you forearm horizontally until you touch the target with the leading edge of your palm. The beauty of this technique is that there is room for error. Even if you are too close, you would still hit the target with your elbow or forearm depending on how close the target is. Always keep elbow slightly bent to prevent injury. A variation of this technique requires that you strike with a closed fist using the bottom of the fist as the striking surface . This technique is called a back Hammer Fist.

Heel Palm Strike

In this technique, the open hand strikes straight forwards onto and slightly upwards against the attacker's nose or chin. The part of the palm close to the wrist known as the heel is the striking surface.

Bring your elbow in close to your side and your hand up in front of your shoulder as though you were going to toss a basketball or shot put. Pull your fingers back and face the palm towards the attacker. Strike by extending your elbow upwards and forwards. You can also get extra power in this technique by first bending your knees slightly and then rising up in conjunction with the strike.

Self Defense Techniques

The following self-defense techniques use a distraction technique first, followed by an escape, then a finishing technique. The most common distraction is a low kick low to the attacker's instep or shin. Escapes often include joint locks to apply pressure to an attacker's joint such as an elbow, wrist, or finger. Forcing the joint against its natural movement will cause pain and if continued can result in a sprain and dislocation. When practicing joint locks it is important to have a stop signal to let your partner know when to stop applying pressure. In Judo this is called 'Tapping Out' and it means that you must tap your partner's arm or shoulder two times to signal them to stop.

Stomp Kick

From a ready stance...

1. The rear (back) leg kicks forwards at shin height.

2. The foot is turned slightly so that the toes point outwards.

The striking surface is the side of the foot.

Back Kick

From a ready stance...

1. The front (lead) leg lifts up with knee bent.

2. The leg then stomps backwards like a donkey.

3. The targets are the shins of someone standing behind you.

Escape from Straight Hand Grab

1) Attacker - Stand in front of your partner and use one hand to grab your partner's wrist.

2) Defender - Distract the attacker by stomp kicking his/her shins.

3) Defender - Do not try to pull away. Move in, bring your body close to the arm being grabbed, and clasp your hands together.

4) Defender - Turn away from the person grabbing you by twisting at the waist and using your whole body to break the grip.

5) Defender - Suddenly reverse the escape move and hit the attacker with a Back Fist strike to the nose.

<u>Tip:</u> Make sure the forearms are kept tight across the abdomen and that you twist your body quickly to escape.

Escape from Double Front Hand Grab

1) Attacker - Stand in front of your partner and use both hands to grab both your partner's wrists.

2) Defender - Distract the attacker by stomp kicking his/her shins.

3) Defender - Move in and bring your body close to one of the arms being grabbed. Turn your body sideways as you step in and bring your arm across your stomach until the attacker's grip on that arm is broken.

4) Defender - Strike sideways towards the attacker's solar plexus using a side elbow.

Tip: Make sure the forearm is kept tight across the abdomen and that you turn sideways or perpendicular to your body.

Escape from Double Hand Grab From Behind

1) Attacker - Stand behind your partner and grab both arms by the wrists.

2) Defender - Step forward with one leg and then use the forward leg to kick back against the attacker's shins until he lets go.

3) Defender - Step forward and bring your elbows up across your chest.

4) Defender - After stepping forward, swing back in either direction and strike with a back elbow aimed at the attacker's jaw or nose.

Tips: This is the simplest technique for this situation. Keep kicking back until the attacker lets go.

Escape from Front Hand Choke

1) Attacker - Stand in front of your partner and put both hands on your partner's throat. Never apply pressure to the throat!

2) Defender - Distract the attacker by stomp kicking his/her shins

3) Defender - Swing one arm over top of the attacker's arms

4) Defender - Simultaneously turn your whole body sideways and bring your upper arm down on the attacker's arms.

5) Defender - Use the same arm to swing back using the bottom of the fist or the elbow as a striking surface aimed against the attacker's nose.

<u>Tips</u>: This technique could easily break someone's nose. Defender should only practice the return blow in slow motion and must stop short.

Escape from Hand Choke From Behind

1) Attacker - Stand behind your partner and gently grab his/her neck from behind.

2) Defender - Lift one arm straight over your head.

3) Defender - Turn in the direction of the raised arm so that your shoulder and body weight press against the attacker's forearms. Turn around completely while bringing your arm down deflecting the attacker's arms away from you.

4) Defender - Finish with a stomp kick to the shins or knee to the groin

<u>Tip</u>: Make sure you turn tight so that you bring your whole body and shoulder against the attacker's forearms.

Escape from Choke from Behind [Arm Bar]

1) Attacker – Grab your partner from behind across the throat using an arm bar. Do not apply any pressure against the throat.

2) Defender - Drop your chin and hunch your shoulders. Stomp on the attacker's instep and kick back against the shins.

3) Defender - Turn in the direction of the attacker's elbow and use the arm closest to the attacker to strike the groin.

4) Defender - Continue to turn towards the attacker's elbow and bring your leg behind the leg closest to you.

5)) Defender - Bring the arm closest to the attacker up and under his chin while using the leg behind the attacker's leg to sweep back throwing the attacker on the ground.

Tip: Escape from an Arm Bar Choke is one of the most difficult escapes. Keep stomping against the shins until the attacker relaxes his grip enough to start turning.

Escape from A Hammerlock

1) Attacker - Stand in front of your partner and use both hands to grab one of your partner's wrists and twist the arm inwards so that your arm is forced up behind your partner's back.

2) Defender - Do not fight against the twisting action. Turn your body around in the direction of the pressure until your arm is across your lower back.

3)) Defender - Turn to face your attacker and use your other hand to push against the attacker's chin

Tip: By turning the body in the direction of the twist, you are able to put the weight of your whole body against the attacker's arm. It is very difficult for the attacker to apply any pressure and so you will not feel any more pain from the hammerlock. In serious situations, instead of a push, strike using the heel of the palm against the attacker's nose.

Escape from Bear Hug from Behind [Under arms]

1) Attacker - Wrap your arms around your partner's waist from behind and under the arms, clasp your hands together.

2) Defender - Use one of your legs to kick back against the attacker's shins.

3) Defender - Clasp your hands together and sink your weight down.

4) Defender - Use two or three back elbow strikes aimed at the jaw in rapid succession alternating from left to right by twisting at the waist.

Tip: Be extra careful in practicing the three back elbows. Go slow since it is easy to hit your partner and cause serious injury. Practice slow motion at first and then increase the speed. The 'Attacker" must lean far back and away to avoid the elbow strikes. Defender must make sure to twist far enough at the waist each time.

Escape from Bear Hug From Behind [Over Arms]

1) Attacker - Wrap your arms over your partner's arms and shoulders from behind and clasp your hands together.

2) Defender _ Use one of your legs to kick back against the attacker's shins.

3) Defender - Raise your arms up in front of your body as if lifting a heavy pail. At the same time, bend your knees and slide down through the attacker's arms.

4) Defender - Use a back elbow to the attacker's stomach.

Tip: Make sure you coordinate lifting the arms with sliding down so that it is one single action. If an attacker is still able to hold on slightly, then use the elbows and the legs to strike back against the attacker until the opportunity to escape.

145

Escape from Front Bear Hug [Under arms]

1) Attacker - Stand in front of your partner and wrap your arms under your partner's arms and around his or her waist.

2) Defender - Use a stomp kick against the attacker's shins or top of the foot.

3) Defender - Cup you palms and slap the attacker's ears.

4) Defender - Bring the heel of your palm up under the attacker's chin or nose and push up and back until he lets go.

Tip: Slapping the ears is an extremely dangerous technique that traps air in the auditory canal and can cause the eardrum to blow. This is also very painful. In practice with a partner, go slowly to avoid trapping the air since even a light slap can be painful. The heel palm to the nose is more painful than to the chin but both are very effective.

Escape from Front Bear Hug [Over arms]

1) Attacker - Stand in front of your partner and wrap your arms around your partner's waist over his or her arms. Clasp your hands together.

2) Defender - Use a knee strike against the attacker's groin.

3) Defender - Simultaneously slide down while lifting your arms. You should be able to bring your hands up behind the attacker's arms, then, using your thumbs, dig them in under the jaw line close to the ears, push up, and back until you break the attacker's hold.

Tip: When learning to dig the thumbs under the jaw line you may have to help your partner on how to position their thumbs to inflict maximum pain. Have your partner apply pressure gradually and do not tap out until you are on the threshold of pain.

Escape from Hair Grab From Behind

1) Attacker - Stand behind your partner and use one hand to grab a hold of his or her hair.

2) Defender - Use both hands to grab the attacker's hand. Press his hand tight to your head

3) Defender - Hold the hand tight to your head, bend forward and turn to face the attacker. His hand should now be palm upwards.

4) Defender - Raise your body up bringing pressure to the attacker's wrist forcing him to stand on his toes.

5) Finish with a stomp to the knee or kick to the groin.

<u>Tip</u>: Done properly you should be able to cause pain in the wrist joint. Go slowly at first and gradually rise up increasing the pressure slowly so that your partner does not get a sprained wrist.

Escape from Side Head Lock

1) Attacker - Stand to the side of your partner and wrap your arm around your partner's neck in a side headlock

2) Defender - Bring the hand closest to the attacker down and behind the attacker. Strike upwards into the attacker's groin

3) Defender - Bring your striking hand back and use both hands to grab the attacker's forearm.

4) Defender - Pull down on the arm and slip your head backwards out of the hold.

5) Maintain your grip on the attacker's forearm then pull up and then forwards executing a hammerlock

<u>Tip</u>: The strike to the groin should succeed in releasing the grip. Remember to practice this one in slow motion.

Chapter 6
Advanced Martial Arts

We tend to stop learning when we have mastered sufficient skills to attain our immediate objective. Thus, for instance, we improve our speech until we can make ourselves understood. But any person who wishes to speak with the clarity of an actor discovers that he must study speech for several years in order to achieve anything approaching his maximum potential. An intricate process of limiting ability accustoms us to make do with a small part of our potential.

Moshe Feldenkrais

Up to this point of the book, the Zen exercises and martial arts techniques are those that anyone can learn easily with the help of a training partner, coach or Orientation and Mobility specialist, and which does not require the supervision of a martial arts expert. However, the martial arts have many more potential benefits for the blind and vision impaired. Unfortunately, to advance beyond the forum of the present work requires a qualified martial arts instructor and one that is patient and open enough to work with the blind. There are many excellent martial arts instructors from numerous styles successfully training the vision impaired and those with other disabilities as well. However, finding such a teacher in your area is not easy. I hope this book will encourage teachers and coaches and provide some basic groundwork that will make such programs more widely available. The following sections are addressed to instructors and those students that are already in an on-going martial arts training program. For the lay reader you might find some of the following useful in deciding whether to seek advanced training.

Forms/*Kata*

A therapy, which encourages expressive movement, increases the motility of the organism, improves its aggression and creates a feeling of strength on both the physical and psychic levels. Alexander Lowen, The Language of the Body

In the martial arts, much time is devoted to learning forms or *Kata* in Japanese. A form is a prearranged series of martial arts techniques similar to a dance routine.

A form contains packets of proprioceptive information such as posture, balance, center of gravity, movement, fluidity, and the transmission of kinetic energy. Martial arts forms have transmitted this information down through dozens of generations. Forms practice is an excellent form of exercise that like dance and gymnastics, places emphasis on developing the senses of proprioception and balance to a much higher degree than other types of sports. As we read in the chapter on Grounding, these two senses contributed greatly to Susan's mobility, navigation, and confidence. With so many benefits to learning forms, should the blind be taught forms? The answer is yes, if possible.

I began teaching Susan the International Wu Shu standard Tai Chi form known as 24 movements. Tai Chi is a Chinese Martial art that is usually performed in 'slow motion' which seemed perfectly suited to blind students and which also emphasizes the Tai Chi Walking exercise mention in the chapter on Grounding. Teaching forms follows the same procedure as teaching the self-defense techniques, by vocal instruction and physically posing the student.

The first problem we encountered was orientation. Depending on the complexity of the form, a student is obliged to make any number of 45, 90, and 180 degree turns. A sighted student would start, for example, by facing the south wall and when it was time to make a 90 degree turn to the right, would end up facing the west wall, simple. Of course, if you cannot see the wall, orienting yourself is more complicated than one would have guessed. As we learned from our walking lesson, humans navigate by landmarks; the answer was simply to create an auditory landmark or in this case an auditory direction beacon.

One simple auditory direction beacon is the musician's metronome. Place the metronome in one area of the room and always begin the form facing the metronome. Then using the tick-tock sound, you should be able to gauge your position in the room with not too much difficulty. Other options could include using a music player or even wind chimes with a fan blowing on them.

I would recommend that when learning forms you always start the form facing the same compass direction. For example, for twenty years I have always started my forms facing south which is traditional in the 'Kung Fu' styles and that is influenced by Chinese mythology which considers south to be the 'lucky' direction. I have noticed that whenever I start my form facing another direction something does not feel right and I tend to make more mistakes.

This may be due to another sense that humans may or may not possess - the sense of magnetic direction. Homing pigeons derive their name from their ability to find their way back to their coops traveling hundreds of miles regardless of where they are released. Scientists have long puzzled how the birds achieved their uncanny navigational abilities. Researchers have discovered that homing pigeons have a molecule of magnetite imbedded deep in the brain and believe that this could enable pigeon, and possibly other species, to sense the earth's magnetic field. [34] Researchers are wondering if a similar particle found in the human brain may also provide information on magnetic currents. [35]

---

[34] *Bird Migration*, Thomas Alerstam, David A. Christie (Translator), Cambridge University Press, 1993

[35] In 1976 Robert Baker, a Zoology professor at Manchester University, conducted an experiment to determine whether magnetic fields affect human

We have seen that navigation and orientation are important skills in mobility. We have learned to use olfactory and auditory landmarks to replace the visual landmarks as a means of navigation for the blind. Is it possible then to have another sense, an eighth sense - the sense of direction?

The ability to sense magnetic fields is described in the strange story of Kaspar Hauser36. As a child Kaspar was kept locked in a cellar without human contact. Upon his sixteenth birthday, he was mysteriously released and later found wandering the streets of Nuremberg. His physician Dr. Daumer records the following abilities: *"He preferred the color red, was so sensitive to food he could only stomach bread and water, even a drop of coffee or wine secretly mixed into his water would cause him to go into sweating convulsions. He was able to tell in repeated experiments whether a*

navigation. Third year Zoology students were blindfolded and driven over a complex and winding route until they were between 6 and 52 km away from Manchester University. First, each student was asked to point towards the university while still blindfolded and then again after removing the blindfold.

Remarkably, they did much better at finding the university when they were blindfolded. This seems to indicate that while blindfolded students were using their 'instinct' rather than trying to work it out from memory or logic.

Then the experiment was repeated but this time the students had little bars of metal strapped around their heads. Half of the little bars were magnets, while the other half were non-magnetic brass, to act as a placebo. The results indicated that students wearing the magnets lost their sense of direction more often. However, the students wearing the non-magnetic brass could still point to the university. This lends credence to the theory that their sense of direction was based on a perception of magnetic fields.

36 Masson, Jeffrey Moussaieff, *Lost Prince: The Unsolved Mystery of Kaspar Hauser*. The Free Press, New York, 1996.

magnet was turned north or south towards him, he described the north as producing a sensation like current of air passing through him."

As Kaspar's intellect and education developed his "Extraordinary, almost preternatural elevation of his senses has sunk almost to a common level."

Again, we see a common pattern with the workings of what can be called the lesser senses, (smell, taste, synesthesia, and direction) that these senses become more acute through isolation, and quiet and through the suppression, or underdevelopment, of personality. Kaspar had almost no human contact and did not know how to speak. Without human interaction he never developed a personality, he may have functioned on an instinctive level similar to the Zen state of mind called 'No-Mind' But as he became educated, civilized, and learned to communicate, these amazing sensory abilities were lost. He developed his mind, but at the expense of his sensory acuity. While Zen teaches that it is necessary to have a personality, it is also necessary to learn how to override this function and tap into the primary sources of information. Other accounts of children found living alone in the wilderness describe similar phenomena. 37 When first discovered they displayed highly accurate senses of smell, taste, hearing, and sight. Then, they

37 *Savage Girls and Wild Boys: A History of Feral Children*, Michael Newton
Thomas Dunne Books, 2003

gradually lost these abilities as they became educated in the ways of the modern world. Therefore, the answer to whether humans may be able to sense direction is a possible yes. Can we train this sense?

If it exists then we should be able to train it using similar principles described before. Tone down other sensory input (Quiet, Isolation, and Relaxation) suppress the personality and its internal dialogue (Inner Calm and Detachment) and try to recognize the feeling of direction. Martial arts teach that before beginning a form you must take a moment to center yourself. All athletes do the same before a game, a shot, a throw, or a lift. This is also a good time to incorporate a brief exercise into the routine as follows:

Centering

Before starting your form, pause for a moment. First, focus on your breathing. Take two or three quick breaths followed by abdominal breathing (See Calming breath). Next, relax; loosen the shoulder and neck muscles, and relax the muscles around the eyes and jaw. Then focus on posture, stand tall but not stiff, limber but not sloppy. Finally, calm your mind and 'Remember' what direction you are facing. Quickly visualize the four directions of the compass. If facing south, then a 90 degrees turn to your right would have you facing west, to the left would be east, and behind you north. Then begin your form.

Another time to incorporate directional training is during the walking lessons. As one goes about mapping auditory and olfactory landmarks, also include the direction relative to the student that these landmarks occur. As we learned earlier, just by becoming aware of certain types of information, trains you to perceive that information more clearly.

So what possible benefits would a sense of direction have for the blind? It may provide a hunch when you are going in the wrong direction when out traveling. Perhaps it could be used in self-defense to 'sense' magnetic fields emanating from other people. Alternatively, it may be that by simply focusing on our subtle senses we encourage the development of that elusive intuition called instinct. It is up to each individual to explore these possibilities and weight the merits. However, since the effort consists of merely thinking about it for a few seconds each time you practice a form, I believe the potential benefits far outweigh the cost.

Therefore, forms can provide numerous benefits for everyone. They are an excellent memory tool, they train your sense of balance and proprioception to the highest degree possible, and they may even be able to refine your innate sense of magnetic direction. The drawback is in the time and effort, as well as the skill of the instructor in teaching the form. With sighted students a form can take anywhere from a few months to a few years to learn. This requires a great deal of dedication by both the teacher and student that may not be feasible in today's fast paced and transient society.

Susan did not succeed in completing the form but this was not due to her blindness. Most sighted students also never complete a form because of the time and effort it takes to learn forms. Susan's failure in this regard is because of the statistical average rather than through disability. Perhaps if Susan had been more physically active in her younger, sighted years she may have been able to learn the form more easily, and therefore derive more satisfaction from it. It is always easier to learn a second musical instrument after you have learned one already. However, as the opening quote suggests, once a person has achieved a certain skill level that meets their needs they seldom go beyond that. Susan had accomplished what she set out to do and the finer skills of forms practice were unnecessary for her. It is for this reason that I believe forms practice to be an advanced skill set that most visually impaired people will not find crucial to becoming a warrior.

Sparring

One who excels as a warrior does not appear formidable; one who excels in defeating the enemy does not join issue. This is known as the virtue of non-contention.
Lao Tzu, *Tao Te Ching*

Simulated hand-to-hand combat is known as sparring, a term used in boxing and sport karate to describe a free form fighting match between two opponents. In the Zatoichi movies, our hero is shown ducking, blocking, and returning sword strikes. Many would seriously doubt that a blind man could fight with such skill. So does this mean that the blind martial artist cannot engage in competitive sparring?

It depends on what type of sparring and under what set of rulest. With point style competitions usually found at Karate and Tae Kwon Do tournaments, the blind are at a distinct disadvantage. However, there are other forms of sparring that allow vision-impaired participants to compete against each other and even other sighted opponents and that allow them to enjoy the benefits of such sportsmanship. The following lists the most suitable styles and types of sparring for those with vision impairment.

Judo

Judo is a Japanese style that focuses on grappling and throwing techniques. Judo contestants start a match by grabbing onto each other's jacket sleeves and then each tries to maneuver his opponent into a throw or trip. The first contestant to bring his or her opponent to the floor wins a point. This form of sparring is ideally suited to the vision impaired since each match begins by making contact with the other contestant. As we learned in the touch sensitivity section, it takes only a little training before a blind person can create an accurate image of the opponent's body position through touch alone. Judo also provides valuable skills that can be used in self-defense applications as well. The only drawback to this form of sparring is that it is quite vigorous and anyone engaging in this activity needs to be in good physical condition. Judo and other grappling oriented styles such as Jujitsu and Aikido all teach sparring forms that are particularly well suited for vision-impaired students, but they also require years of study under a competent teacher.

Self-defense/Randori

Randori is a Japanese term that means "chaos taking" and refers to free-style practice or sparring. The exact meaning of Randori depends on the martial art. In some styles, it refers to one-on-one free form sparring of the type most commonly seen at Karate tournaments. In other styles, it refers to a form of practice in which a student defends against multiple attackers in quick succession without knowing how they will attack, or in what order. This form of Randori is not free form sparring, and the attackers are not allowed to resist or counter the defender's techniques.

This type of sparring is often seen at martial arts tournaments and often sighted contestants are blindfolded, showing that they do not need to rely on vision to be effective. There are slight variations on what rules are used, but usually the contestant/defender stands in the middle of the mat while several other opponents run up and engage the defender in a hold. The defender escapes and counters and then waits for the next attacker and so on for between 3 to 5 attacks. The contestant is judged on form, intensity, effectiveness, realism, and execution of technique.

Randori is also an excellent training exercise for self-defense skills proficiency. All of the self-defense techniques described in the previous chapter can be used to train in this fashion. On the occasions that I brought Susan to the local Karate club, I had several karate students volunteer to attack Susan in Randori. After several months of training Susan was able to defend against up to eight attacks one after the other in a matter of seconds. Randori is also less vigorous than Judo, which makes it accessible to people with a wider variety of physical conditions.

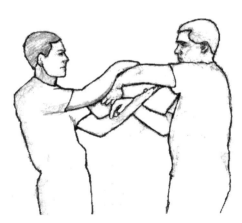

Sticky Hands

Sticky Hands is the name of a principal in Chinese styles known as sticking-to-your-opponent. It also refers to a type of free form sparring. Again, there are variations in execution but the basic

practice is as follows. Opponents stand facing each other with arms extended and in contact with each other's arms touching forearm to forearm close to the wrists. Without breaking contact, both contestants circle their arms using both a clockwise and counter-clockwise circling motion. (I.e. while your right arm circles clockwise, your left arm circles counter-clockwise and vice versa) While circling the arms, each contestant maintains contact through their forearms in effect 'sticking' to each other. After three circles, either contestant is then free to launch an attack. The trick is to sense and then 'Jam' (interfere) with the opponent's attack while launching you own counter-attack. For example, if your opponent intends to strike using his right hand you should be able to sense the attack through your contact with his right forearm. Your left forearm would 'stick' to his and as he attacks, you would use your left arm to deflect the attack away from you.

When a point is scored, or the attack ends in a stalemate, then the contest begins again with the three circling hands. Sighted students, when reaching advanced levels, practice this exercise while blindfolded to develop sticking ability and improve touch sensitivity.

So what exactly is this sticking ability? There is an old story about a Tai Chi master who would demonstrate his sticking ability as follows. He had a bird trained to perch on his finger. With a nudge, the bird would fly around and then land again on the master's finger. However, when the master used his sticking ability the bird could not leave his finger. The trick is in knowing the flight and takeoff characteristics of birds. Before taking off, the bird will drop down while raising his wings, and then jump up and flap his wings downwards. The Tai Chi master was able to sense the exact moment when the bird would drop its weight and raise his finger to perfectly counter the bird's motion and cancel the bird's momentum, thus preventing the bird from flying away. The principle of Sticky Hands is common to most martial arts whereby each contestant tries to sense what his opponent is intending to do and then counter his momentum to negate the attack.

This is a safe exercise and does not require intense physical training but if attacks to the head are allowed, then full face and head protection is required.

Push Hands

Push Hands is an exercise taught in the Tai Chi styles and is a mild form of sparring. There are several variations and levels of difficulty. In the simplest version known as Single Push Hands two contestants stand facing each other with the same foot forward. Contestants then extend their lead hands with palms outwards and wrists slightly bent back. Just as in the Sticky Hands exercise, contestants maintain contact with each other's arms by hooking the back of their wrists with each other. Again, the contestants make a circling motion with their arms but this time it is a horizontal circle like stirring a large pot. At any time, either opponent can attempt to push or pull his opponent off balance. For example, with right hands connecting, as I circle my right hand towards my opponent I direct my palm towards his chest in an attempt to push him off balance. My opponent would sense the attack, then absorb and redirect my momentum away from him. If I over extend myself past my center of gravity, I will risk losing balance and fall forward instead. Whoever loses balance first loses the point. The purpose of the exercise is to learn how to absorb and redirect energy so that anyone attacking you would feel like he or she was trying to submerge a beach ball with one hand. The more downward pressure you apply, the more likely the ball will roll up and out of your grasp. Almost anyone can do this very safe exercise. Although push hands appears very simple, there are dozens of books dedicated to expounding all the variations and subtleties and thus requires the assistance of an experienced teacher to learn.

With the exception of Judo, which would have been too physically demanding, Susan quickly learned these sparring methods, which added greatly to her self-confidence. To feel confident in their ability to defend themselves, all students will benefit from experience gained in applying their knowledge against another opponent. Through sparring, the vision impaired can test and develop their abilities to; sense through touch, anticipate actions, perceive attack patterns, remain balanced under stress, evade, absorb, redirect, and counter-attack. While most of the above sparring exercises are easy to learn, they do require a knowledgeable teacher and strict supervision since no amount of verbal description can adequately convey the dynamic and subtle physical movements involved.

Training Tips

Trainers need to first consider each student's physical abilities and judge what they are able to do safely before teaching sparring exercises. Start off by having a sighted training partner spar with your vision-impaired student until the techniques become comfortable, only after everyone feels confident with the exercises should vision impaired students be paired together. Begin each type of sparring by performing the action first in slow motion. Once the basics are mastered, bring the level up to full speed.

Weapons

Well then, the accomplished man uses the sword but does not kill others. He uses the sword and gives others life. When it is necessary to kill, he kills. When it is necessary to give life, he gives life.

Takuan Soho, Letter to Yagyu Munenori

The inevitable question that arises when learning martial arts and self-defense is the use of weapons. For the vision impaired, an obvious choice in trying to even the odds in a criminal encounter is to be armed. As a rule, a weapon is preferable to empty hand in a struggle for survival. However, carrying a weapon for self-defense has several drawbacks. The first drawback is accessibility. There is little likelihood that you will be able to retrieve the weapon from a purse, pocket, boot, or waistband fast enough. Criminals know to use the element of surprise when assailing someone giving the intended victim no time to go for a weapon.

Another drawback is the skill required to use a weapon effectively. Under the stress of combat, even a handgun can have limited effectiveness. While traditional martial arts weapons such as *Nunchakus, Kobutans*, and *Tonfas* appear lethal in the Dojo, under the stress of a street fight they can be awkward and difficult to handle menacing both attacker and wielder. Irritant sprays, firearms, and knives would have limited effectiveness for the vision impaired.

The third drawback to carrying a weapon is the legal ramifications. In most countries, carrying a concealed weapon is illegal and the penalties for carrying a concealed weapon can be serious. Even if you are attacked, and you use the weapon only in defense, you will find yourself under suspicion because carrying a weapon implies that you must have had the intention to use violence. The attacker may successfully sue you for medical and other costs even if he had provoked the attack.

Given the numerous drawbacks and limited advantages, carrying a concealed weapon has little use in self-defense. Despite the unfeasibility of traditional weapons training for the blind, the question remained, would learning the use of a weapon offer Susan an advantage in a self-defense situation? I decided we should train using the sword's poor cousin – the short staff or *Jo.*

The Jo is the quintessential Zen weapon; simple, utilitarian, and versatile. It combines techniques of both the sword and the staff. Although humble in appearance, the Jo is famous in Japan as the only weapon to defeat the famed swordsman Miyamoto Musashi. In an earlier match with a simple farmer named Muso Gonnasuke (1584-1645) who was armed with a *Bo* (six foot staff) Musashi was the victor but spared the farmer's life. Determined to win the next time, Gonnasuke retired to the mountains to devise and perfect techniques that would defeat Musashi's famous two sword style. During a revelation, Gonnasuke was inspired to shorten the Bo to approximately four feet in length. With this new weapon, which he named the Jo, he was able to defeat Musashi, and in turn spared his life for the earlier favour. Gonnasuke went on to found the *Jo Jiutsu* style still practiced to this day.

The short staff is truly versatile and most people have an intuitive grasp of how to use it which makes learning this weapon easier. I first taught Susan self-defense applications using the Jo. All of the previously described self-defense techniques were adapted and proved even more effective and devastating. For example, using a two handed grip and employing a basic clothesline technique, the Jo could ward off and break almost any type of attack or hold.

Susan was also able to learn how to twirl the staff in a downward figure eight pattern and, using her hearing, was able to chase me around the room while whirling the weapon threateningly in front of her. As mentioned previously we also practiced using a pair of padded sticks and safety helmets with sometimes surprising results

Since the Jo and the white cane are similar in length it would appear that the folding White Cane would make a ready weapon, but the lightweight aluminum construction is not solid enough to survive such rough handling. Unfortunately, a Jo's weight and bulk makes it uncomfortable to carry in the manner in which the white cane is used. However, skill in handling one can translate well into skill handling the other and so this provides another benefit in training with a Jo.

There are forms or Katas that employ the short staff and which vision impaired students could learn. Today, Jo training is taught almost exclusively in Aikido schools although some Karate and Kung Fu styles have short staff forms and in either case could adapt both Long Staff and Sword techniques to the short staff.

Although weapons have little practical use in modern self-defense, they open another avenue of training for the blind and vision impaired and provides the same benefits as forms training does.

Tips for Trainers

Teaching weapons forms and routines follows the same steps as for any form. Take extra care to insure that the area is clear of obstructions, that students practice far enough apart, and that no one should wander within range of anyone's practice. If teaching self-defense techniques, then use a padded and flexible staff and the 'Attacker' or *Uke* should wear protective equipment. A solid oak staff is a dangerous weapon and should not be used for practicing self-defense applications since even a small mistake could result in serious injury.

Conclusion

I trained Susan for about eight months and I was amazed at her improvement. Susan was not able to develop superhuman perceptions or super powers as portrayed in the movies, but that was never really the point. She had come to me because she was afraid and she felt helpless. Learning self-defence showed her that she was not as helpless as she thought which helped reduce her fear.

Susan was probably the least likely candidate for martial arts instruction, blind, approaching middle age, out of shape and overweight. Most people would feel too daunted by the physical disadvantages to attempt such learning yet Susan had incredible courage to seek out a martial arts instructor and take lessons. More than anything, it is that kind of bravery that made her successes possible.

When we first started her training I asked Susan about her social life. She said she did not have much of a social life but she had heard that the Toronto Association for the Blind held monthly singles dances and she had always wanted to go. Her lack of self-confidence prevented her from going. When I last spoke with her, she was on her way to the dance.

"Aren't you nervous?" I teased her.

"After kicking your ass around the gym for the last eight months, dancing will be a breeze."

I'm sure it was.

Afterword

The events in this book took place in 1990, and long before the internet. Before training Susan, I had spoken with a couple of people that worked at different blind associations, but unfortunately, they provided me with little useful information at that time. One thing neither Susan nor I were even aware of was the Orientation and Mobility field. Only after publication of this book did I correspond with O&M specialists and learn about this useful field of study.

Much of our work, I realize now, would fall under the heading of Orientation and Mobility rather than martial arts. For example, the Walking Lessons we devised, are very similar to the basis of O&M training.

At that time, I had no experience working with the blind. I approached Susan's needs from the point of view of a martial arts teacher. That the solutions we discovered were so similar to the solutions employed by O&M specialists, suggests that martial arts' training is compatible with any O&M program.

Also since writing this book, I have corresponded with dozens of blind martial arts students and teachers from around the world. I have also collected news clippings of blind martial artists who successfully defended themselves against muggers and rapists.

Being a natural skeptic, I was careful not to make any outrageous claims regarding martial arts training for the blind. However, in light of information I have received since then, I feel confident that the benefits Susan received are readily available to other blind martial arts students. Indeed, many blind martial artists have developed skills exceeding the claims made in this book.

In conclusion, I believe martial arts are by far the most beneficial form of physical activity any blind or vision-impaired person could choose to pursue.

Glossary of Martial Arts Styles

Kung Fu: (Skillfulness) Originated in China and is up to three thousand years old. It is called the grandfather of martial arts because many other countries such as Japan and Korea borrowed heavily from Chinese Kung Fu when developing their own systems. Kung Fu styles generally emphasize punching and striking techniques but most styles teach grappling and throwing techniques as well.

Karate-Do: (The way of the empty hand) Originated in Okinawa and is up to 1600 years old. The early founders of Okinawa Te (Okinawa Hand) had learned the Shaolin style from Chinese traders. Gichen Funakoshi brought the art to Japan in 1922 where it became very popular. Karate Do is more direct and linear than Kung Fu. The Japanese knack for efficiency worked to streamline the traditional Kung Fu styles into it efficient components. Karate emphasizes punch and kick techniques but also includes grappling and joint locking techniques.

Ju jitsu: (Pliable techniques) Originated in Japan and is actually a broad term used to designate any one of hundreds of schools many dating back some 1,600 years. Thought to have developed out of peasant hand-to-hand combat techniques used against armored warriors, Ju-Jitsu has a reputation for no-nonsense applications. Ju jitsu styles teach a broad range techniques and weapons with an emphasis on grappling, joint locking, and throwing techniques.

Judo: (The way of yielding) Judo is the direct descendant of Jujitsu. After the abolition of the Samurai (Warrior) class in 1867, many Japanese martial arts systems mad38e a transition into more sport oriented forms. The founder of modern Judo, Jigoro Kano, adapted Jujitsu and removed striking and joint locking techniques to create a safer competitive sports style. Jigoro also invented the colored belt grading system used in most martial arts schools. Judo consists entirely of throwing techniques although many teachers will also teach grappling and joint locks, as an adjunct to the sports training.

Aikido: (The way of spiritual union) Originated in Japan and may be up to 1200 years old. Morihei Ueshiba (1883-1969) is the founder of modern Aikido. He transformed the deadly techniques of earlier Aiki-jujitsu into a more peaceful art that emphasizes harmony and yielding with the attack. This style is comprised of mostly grappling, throwing, and joint locking techniques. Aikido also teaches both Katana (Japanese saber) and Jo (short staff) arts.

Tae Kwon Do: (The Way of the Foot and Fist) is a modern Korean style that evolved out of earlier systems that date as far back as the 7th century. Modern Tae Kwon Do is best known for its spectacular aerial kicks. Emphasis is on punching and kicking techniques although grappling techniques are taught at higher levels.

Tai Chi: (Supreme Energy Fist) Originated in China and is one of the 'internal' Kung Fu styles. Tai Chi Chuan is performed much slower than other styles and the emphasis is on relaxation and concentration. It is characterized by its flowing movement and calmness. Emphasis is mostly on health and spiritual benefits but also includes some effective grappling and striking techniques.

Bibliography

Ackerman, Diane, *A Natural History of the Senses*, Random House, New York, 1990, 152. 1 Ack

Alexander, John B., Grollier, Richard, Morris, Janet, *The Warrior's Edge*, William Morrow & Co., New York, 1990.

Cleary, Thomas, *Vitality Energy Spirit; a Taoist Sourcebook*, Shambala Publications, Boston, 1991.

Chogyam, Trungpa, *Shambala, The Sacred Path of the Warrior*, Shambala Publications, Boston, 1984,

Cytowic, Richard E. M.D., *The Man Who Tasted Shapes*, Jeremy P. Thathcher/Putnam Books, New York, 1993,

Deshimaru, Taisen, *The Zen Way To The Martial Arts*, E.P. Dutton, New York, 1982

Draeger, Donn F., *Ninjitsu, The Art of Invisibility*, Yen books, Japan, 1989.

Eliade, Mircea, *Yoga; Immortality and Freedom*, Princeton University Press.

Evans-Wentz, W. Y., EDT., *Tibetan Yoga and Secret Doctrines*, Oxford University Press, London, 1958.

Goldstein, Bruce E., *Sensation and Perception*, Wadsworth Publishing, Belmont, Cal. 1989.

Grof, Stanislav, *The Holotropic Mind*, Harper, San Francisco, S.F.,1990.

Howes, David, Edt. *The Varieties Of Sensory Experience*, University of Toronto Press, Toronto, Can, 1991.

Le Querer, Annick, *Scent, The Mysterious and Essential Powers Of Smell*, Turtle Bay Books, New York, 1992.

Louis, David, Edt. *2001 Fascinating Facts,* Wing Books, New York, 1983.

Murphy, Michael, *The Future of the Body, Explorations Into the Further Evolution of Human Nature*, Putnam Books, New York, 1992.

Musashi, Miyamoto, *The Book Of Five Rings,* Bantam Books, New York, 1982

(The) Mystifying Mind, Library of Curious and Unusual Facts, Time Life books, Alexandria Virginia, 1991.

Reps, Paul, Compiler, *Zen Flesh, Zen Bones* Double day, Anchor Books, Garden City, N. Y., private

Restak, Richard M., *Receptors*, Bantam Books, New York, 1994.

Restak, Richard M., *The Mind*, Bantam Books, New York, 1988.

Sekida, Katsuki, *Zen Training, Methods and Philosophy*, Weatherhill, New York, 1985.

Shosan, Susuki, *Warrior Of Zen*, Translated by Arthur Braverman, Kodansha International, New York, 1994.

Smith, Jillyn, *Senses and Sensibilities*, Wiley Science Editions, New York, 1989.

Soho, Takuan, Translator; William Scott Wilson, *The Unfettered Mind, Writings of the Zen Master to the Sword Master*, Kodansha International, Tokyo, 1986.

Soho, Takuan, *The Unfettered Mind, Writings of the Zen Master to the Sword Master*, Translator; William Scott Wilson, Kodansha International, Tokyo, 1986.

Speads, Carola, *Ways to Better Breathing*, Healing Arts Press, Vermont, 1978.

Sternbach, Richard A., *Mastering Pain. A Twelve Step Program For Coping with Chronic Pain*, G.P. Putnam & Sons, New York, 1987.

Susuki, Shunryu, *Zen Mind, Beginner's Mind*, Weatherhill Press, New York, 1970.

Tsunetomo, Yamamoto, Translator. William Scott Wilson, *Hagakure, The Book of the Samurai*, Avon Books, New York, 1979.

Yokoi, Yuho, *Zen Master Dogen*, Weatherhill, New York, 1976.

Zong Wu & LI Mao, *Ancient Way To Keep Fit*, Shelter Publications, California, 1990.

Index

Aikido, 30, 161, 169, 173
Aldous Huxley, 95, 116
Alexander Lowen, 21, 152
anxiety, 38, 46, 55, 62, 103, 116, 117, 124, 127
Audio Calibration, 61, 66
auditory, 52, 58, 59, 60, 61, 62, 63, 64, 65, 67, 69, 71, 80, 82, 88, 131, 146, 153, 155, 158
Back Kick, 136
Bamboo Breathing, 114, 115
biofeedback, 61, 89, 122
Bo, 14, 168
Bodhidharma, 14
body language, 23, 24
Braille, 12
Buddhism, 13, 14, 94
Bushido, 16
Centering, 157
chemical senses, 72, 75
Chi Kung, 110
Chuang Tzu, 97
Classical Conditioning, 25, 118
detachment, 93, 94, 95
Detachment, 93, 157
diabetes, 11
electromagnetic, 60
emotional state, 25
endocrine system, 104
endorphins, 59
Endorphins, 104
Escape from a Hammerlock, 143
Escape from Bear Hug from Behind, 144, 145

Escape from Choke from Behind, 142
Escape from Double Front Hand Grab, 138
Escape from Double Hand Grab From Behind, 139
Escape from Front Bear Hug, 146, 147
Escape from Front Hand Choke, 140
Escape from Hair Grab from Behind, 148
Escape from Hand Choke from Behind, 141
Escape from Side Head Lock, 149
Escape from Straight Hand Grab, 137
Extended Hearing Exercise, 96
Extending Hearing Exercise, 68
fear, 12, 13, 19, 38, 39, 55, 72, 73, 80, 101, 102, 103, 104, 105, 106, 107, 108, 109, 113, 116, 117, 123, 124, 125, 126, 171
Fight or Flight, 103, 110
grappling, 129, 160, 172, 173, 174
Grounding, 19, 20, 21, 34, 35, 152, 153
Hammer Fist, 134
Heel Palm Strike, 135
Helen Keller, 17, 52, 72
Herman Hesse, 55
hippocampus, 74

Holding the Jug, 28, 112
Horse Stance, 29, 31
hyperosmia, 71, 73
hyperventilation, 109, 111
hypothalamus, 74
Inference, 91
Inner Calm, 98, 157
Jo, 168, 169, 173
Jo Jiutsu, 168
Judo, 135, 160, 162, 165, 173
Karate, 33, 160, 161, 162,
    169, 172
Kaspar Hauser, 155
Kata, 94, 152
landmarks, 64, 82, 153, 155,
    158
Lao Tzu, 14, 100, 159
magnetic direction, 154, 158
Mantra, 59, 99
Mantras, 99
Mark Twain, 108
Meditation, 96, 115
Miyamoto Musashi, 30, 105,
    168
Moshe Feldenkrais, 151
mucosa, 74, 77, 79
Muso Gonnasuke, 168
nervous system, 25, 38, 42,
    56, 59, 60, 96, 98, 103, 104,
    105, 106, 110
Nietzsche, 71
Ninja, 11, 50
Olfaction, 71
olfactory bulb, 74, 79
orientation, 153, 155
panic attacks, 13
parapsychology, 84
parasympathetic system, 105,
    106, 109
Perception, 53, 71, 74, 175

Perceptual Set, 91
posture, 15, 20, 21, 22, 23, 24,
    25, 26, 27, 28, 29, 32, 34,
    42, 43, 46, 54, 152, 157
proprioception, 27, 35, 39, 41,
    42, 43, 47, 88, 152, 158
Push Hands, 164
Pythagoras, 62
Randori, 161, 162
Relaxation, 116, 121, 157
Releasing the Bowstring, 120
Rhythmic Breathing, 113
self- defence, 12
Self Fulfilling Prophesy, 92
seventh sense, 88, 89
Shaolin, 15, 172
Shunryu Susuki, 95
Shunryu Suzuki, 21, 110
Siddhartha, 13, 55
Siddhartha Gautama, 13
sixth sense, 50
Sparring, 159
Stanislav Grov, 86
Sticky Hands, 162, 164
Stomp Kick, 136
Stop Exercise, 19, 34, 38
strategy, 24, 50, 105, 108
Sun Tzu, 105, 129
Suski Shosan, 13
sympathetic system, 105, 106,
    109
synesthesia, 87, 89, 156
synesthetic, 87
Systematic De-sensitization,
    122
Tae Kwon Do, 160, 173
Tai Chi, 28, 32, 34, 45, 97,
    153, 163, 164, 174
Takuan Soho, 85, 166
Tao, 14, 100, 159

Taoism, 14, 100
Taoists, 24
thalamus, 74
The Art of Seeing, 95, 116
The Art of War, 129
The Seventh Sense, 60, 83
Touch Sensitivity Exercise, 132
Tracking, 80, 81
Urbok Vita disease, 102
vestibular system, 39, 40
Walking Lesson, 63, 126
Walking Lessons, 82

Weapons, 166
Weber's Law, 96
white cane, 12, 126, 169
Yagyu Munenori, 9
Yogis, 24
Zatoichi, 9, 11
Zazen, 15, 90, 110
Zen, 1, 2, 3, 13, 14, 15, 16, 17, 19, 21, 26, 39, 65, 84, 86, 89, 90, 92, 93, 94, 95, 99, 110, 115, 151, 156, 168, 175, 176

About the Author

Stefan H. Verstappen is a Canadian writer, adventurer, and martial artist. He has worked as a wilderness survival instructor for Outward Bound programs, a street youth counselor, a First Aid and CPR instructor for St John Ambulance, and a martial arts instructor. He is a world traveler and spent four years living in the Orient.

For more information on the author visit: www.chinastrategies.com

Other Books by Stefan Verstappen

The Art of Urban Survival,
A Family Safety and Self Defense Manual
The complete guide to survival in the concrete jungle. The modern urban environment is rife with dangers. Crime, violence, natural disasters, wars, and terrorism are real life possibilities for which few people are prepared.
Woodbridge Press, 2011, Toronto
http://www.chinastrategies.com/survival.htm
ISBN 978-0-9869515-0-3

The Thirty-Six Strategies of Ancient China
The Thirty-Six Strategies is a unique collection of ancient Chinese proverbs that describe some of the most cunning and subtle strategies ever devised. These proverbs describe not only battlefield strategies, but tactics used in psychological warfare to undermine both the enemy's will to fight - and his sanity
China Books & Periodicals, SF, 1999,
www.chinastrategies.com/home36
ISBN-10: 0835126420
ISBN-13: 978-0835126427

Chinese Business Etiquette:
The Practical Pocket Guide,
This essential pocket reference on common business and social protocols for traveling and doing business in China, Taiwan, and Hong Kong, is ideal for anyone doing business with the Chinese, at home or abroad.
Stone Bridge, Press, Berkeley, 2008
www.chinastrategies.com/cbe.htm
 ISBN-10: 1933330635
ISBN-13: 978-1933330631